Praise for *Fast Forward* . . .

"Powerfully outlines the key drivers for success in business today...Successful executives of the future will find LeBoeuf's book a very valuable and simple tool as they strategically position themselves."
—Roger Milliken, Chairman and CEO,
Milliken & Company

"Hits the mark with many action-ready ideas that will help any company master its future."
—Bill Williams, President and CEO,
TEC—An International Organization of CEOs

"We all want to do it better, cheaper, faster. *Fast Forward* has the support systems to allow us to accomplish it."
—Horst H. Schulze, President and CEO, The Ritz-Carlton Hotel Company;
Malcolm Baldridge National Quality Award-Winner

"Hits the nail on the head! It's as timely as the morning news and as practical as a button on a shirt."
—B. J. Cline, Vice-Chairman of the Board,
Alexander & Alexander, Inc.

"Elegant in its simplicity, yet profound in its implication for business and our way of life. It provides a very comprehensive view of what businesses have to do today to be successful in the changing times of tomorrow."
—Charles E. Whalen, Jr., President and CEO,
Warren Featherbone Company

Berkley Books by Michael LeBoeuf, Ph.D.

IMAGINEERING

HOW TO WIN CUSTOMERS AND KEEP THEM FOR LIFE

GETTING RESULTS!

FAST FORWARD

▲

FAST FORWARD

HOW TO WIN A LOT MORE BUSINESS IN A LOT LESS TIME

▼

Michael LeBoeuf, Ph.D.

B
BERKLEY BOOKS, NEW YORK

FAST FORWARD: HOW TO WIN A LOT MORE
BUSINESS IN A LOT LESS TIME

A Berkley Book / published by arrangement with
the author

PRINTING HISTORY
G. P. Putnam's Sons edition / January 1994
Berkley trade paperback edition / March 1995

ISBN: 0-425-14613-8

BERKLEY®
Berkley Books are published by The Berkley Publishing Group,
200 Madison Avenue, New York, New York 10016.
BERKLEY and the "B" design
are trademarks belonging to Berkley Publishing Corporation.

PRINTED IN THE UNITED STATES OF AMERICA

10 9 8 7 6 5 4 3 2 1

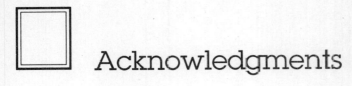 # Acknowledgments

With special thanks to:

Artie and Richard Pine for many years of loyalty, enthusiasm, friendship, and wise guidance of my writing career.

Roger Cooper, Donna Gould, and Rena Wolner for their enthusiastic support.

Steve Ross for editing the manuscript and providing a valuable second pair of eyes.

Neil Baum, Deanna Berg, John Gremer, Jim Hannah, Ian and Pat Huntley, Miriam Piccinini, Tony Richards, Ed Rigsbee, Robert Tucker, Mark Sanborn, Jeff Slutsky, Gus Whalen, and Ron Wright, and the numerous companies and executives who contributed to this book by sharing their ideas and experiences.

 Dedication

To all the readers of my books, the listeners and viewers of my audio and video programs, and the companies and professional associations that have invited me to speak. *Thank you for the privilege of allowing me to have such an interesting and enjoyable career.*

 Contents

Something to Think About   9

Introduction—Speed Is Profit   11

THE TEN COMMANDMENTS OF SPEED

1. Focus on the Customer   19
2. Get In Step With the Future   34
3. Be an Innovator   53
4. Do It With Quality   76
5. Get Rapid, Accurate Feedback   94
6. Ability Means Agility   120
7. If It Doesn't Add Value, Don't Do It   135
8. Build Teams, Not Empires   146
9. Lifelong Learning Is Everybody's Job   166
10. Just Do It!—Now!   189

A Final Thought   207

Postscript   209

Index   211

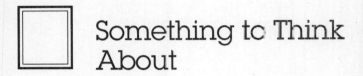

Something to Think About

If you take a normal, healthy frog and throw him into a pot of boiling water, he quickly jumps out. However, if you place the frog in a pot of water at room temperature, and very slowly heat the water one degree at a time, he passively floats in the water and literally allows himself to be boiled alive. Unfortunately, too many people in business today respond to changing times much like the boiled frog. They act as if change doesn't exist in the hope that maybe it will all go away.

Did you know that the average life span of a Fortune 500 company is only 40 years and shrinking?

Are you aware that over 50 percent of the 1980 Fortune 500 companies had vanished from the list by 1993?

Are you and your employer doing what it's going to take to survive and prosper in an even more turbulent future, or are you passively croaking as the water slowly heats?

Read on and find out.

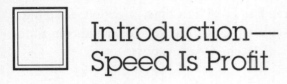

Introduction—
Speed Is Profit

The test of a merchant is how responsive he or she is to change. And if one isn't sensitive to that and doesn't respond to what's going on in the industry, they are going to get killed.

—EDWARD BRENNAN, CEO, Sears

When asked how today's turbulent business world is affecting his life, a corporate CEO replied, "I sleep like a baby. Every three hours I wake up and cry."

Sweeping changes are drastically changing the playing field and the rules for success in business. What's causing it? In a word, technology. Technology is shrinking time and space, giving customers more choices and businesses more competition with less time to respond. If you acknowledge the results of technology, you have taken the first step to a successful future. But if you ignore it, you may be courting economic disaster.

This book presents an exciting, new, action-ready approach to getting better, faster results in a business world where swift, unpredictable change has become the status quo. The purpose of this book is to teach you how to adapt to, initiate, and capitalize on change rather than become a victim of it. And what you need to know and practice can be summed up in a single word—SPEED.

Why speed? Because in today's turbulent business environment, the most profitable businesses are the ones that anticipate and react most quickly to customers' wants. "Time is money" may have been true in Ben Franklin's time, but "Speed is profit" is the new business axiom that will make people and companies rich for the foreseeable future. Here's why:

• *Speed gives you the initial edge in the market.* Being the first to meet customer desires gives a business an initial dominance in the market. Being the first company to produce a personal computer enabled an upstart like Apple to compete with giants the size of IBM.

• *Speed reduces risk.* The faster a business can meet customer wants, the less the odds of the customer's changing his mind or buying elsewhere.

• *Speed increases revenue* because customers willingly pay premium prices for fast service. The success of Federal Express in the eighties is a classic example. We are living in an era characterized by customers and businesses that are time poor. They will gladly pay for not having to wait. Today, overnight mail services are being challenged by the fax machine that is even faster (and in many cases cheaper).

• *Speed increases market share.* Promising and delivering fast service can capture a large share of the market. Case in point, Domino's Pizza.

• *Speed and quality go hand in hand.* The fastest way to deliver a product or service is to do it right the first time. And higher quality increases revenues, lowers costs, builds worker pride, and creates loyal customers.

• *Speed increases efficiency.* A restaurant that learns to turn over its tables twice as fast stands to double its revenue. At the same time, it incurs little or no additional increases in fixed overhead costs such as rent, utilities, and salaries.

• *Speed shrinks expensive inventory costs and the need to rely on market forecasts.* The fastest manufacturers can make and ship an order the same day. And retailers with quick-response order systems enjoy higher inventory turnovers with less investment.

• *Speed improves morale* because employees are working for a more successful, responsive company. Speed also forces management to give them more autonomy and flexibility.

• *Speed creates an innovative edge.* Speeding up (shortening) the product-development cycle enables a business to bring out more new and improved products. The cumulative effect is that the business with a shorter product-development cycle gets products on the market that are years ahead of the competition. And the highest, state-of-the-art products command premium prices.

• *Speed pays even when things go wrong.* Seventy percent of customers who complain will do business with you again if you resolve the complaint to their satisfaction. But if you resolve it on the spot, 95 percent will do business with you again.

In short, success in today's rapidly changing business world requires moving quickly. This doesn't mean pushing yourself and others to work at an overstressed, breakneck pace. There's already much too much of that. But it does mean taking a whole new focus and approach to working, selling, managing, and leading to speed up the business.

For the past several years I have been doing research, consulting, and talking to businesses in an effort to find what works and what doesn't in an era of accelerating change. Whether it's GE or Motorola in manufacturing, Wal-Mart or Home Depot in retailing, or Southwest Airlines in the service sector, thriving businesses and their employees are practicing ten key essentials. I call them the ten commandments of speed. They are:

1. *Focus on the Customer*—He signs everybody's paycheck.
2. *Get in Step With the Future*—That's where opportunity lies.
3. *Be an Innovator*—In an era of rapid change, continuous improvement through innovation is king.
4. *Do It With Quality*—It lowers costs, increases speed, builds pride, and improves customer loyalty.
5. *Get Rapid, Accurate Feedback*—Know what your customers, competitors, employees, suppliers, and the market are doing. Ignorance can be fatal.
6. *Ability Means Agility*—Be flexible and quick to respond and adapt.
7. *If It Doesn't Add Value, Don't Do It*—Any job or activity that doesn't build value is creating needless overhead. Don't do it or get rid of it.
8. *Build Teams, Not Empires*—Cross-functional work teams make better, faster decisions than bureaucracies.
9. *Lifelong Learning Is Everybody's Job*—If you want to stay gainfully employed in a rapidly changing world, learn how to learn and keep learning.
10. *Just Do It!—Now!*—Set challenging deadlines that force yourself and others to use time in the most efficient and effective manner.

In this book you'll find chapters on each of the ten commandments of speed with specific, action-ready ideas for putting them to work. These chapters contain valuable information for owners, managers, salespersons, and anyone who works and wants to prosper in the new economy.

In a world where speed is profit, I promise not to waste your time with excess verbiage. My goal is to give you as much useful information as possible on every page and make it as interesting and entertaining as possible. To get the most from this book, I recommend the following:

1. Read the book slowly but thoroughly the first time with a pencil, pen, or highlighter in your hand. Highlight key passages and make notes to yourself in the margin. If you run across a particularly useful idea, dog-ear the page or write the page number in the front of the book.
2. After you have read the entire book, spend a few minutes at the start of each work day paging through the book, noting the highlights you marked. The key to applying useful knowledge is to get it ingrained in your subconscious, and you accomplish that through spaced repetition.
3. Try to come up with one new way each day for applying a concept or idea that you particularly like.
4. If you are an owner or manager, share this information with your people at work. Better yet, if you like the book, get everyone a copy. Then challenge each person to come up with at least ten new ideas for applying the ten commandments of speed in their job. If everyone at work implements just one new idea to speed up their work, the cost of the book will be insignificant when compared to the benefits. Just imagine the impact of ten, or twenty, or more ideas.
5. Make something happen! Put the new ideas into action in your own job and encourage others to do the same. Have everyone, yourself included, keep a log and record incidents of what's actually being done to speed up the business. Encourage everyone to share their incidents, ideas, and problems, and give them plenty of positive recognition and praise when they do.

Today's turbulent business world is like a fast-moving card game. Every day we are dealt varying combinations of aces, deuces, jokers, and everything in between. To be sure, some hands are better than others. But every good card player knows that success isn't the result of the hand you're dealt but how you play the hand. In business, speed is your trump card. It raises revenue, lowers costs, complements quality, kills the competition, and customers love it.

When discussing football, the late legendary coach, Paul "Bear" Bryant said, "Luck follows speed." I can't think of a better prescription for success in the present and future world of business. So let's get started with the first and most important commandment of speed. On your marks, get set, READ!

THE TEN COMMANDMENTS OF SPEED

Every morning in Africa, a gazelle wakes up knowing it must run faster than the fastest lion or be killed. Every morning a lion awakens knowing it must outrun the slowest gazelle or starve to death. It doesn't matter if you are a lion or a gazelle. When the sun comes up, you'd better be running.

—ANONYMOUS

1 Focus on the Customer

There is only one boss. The customer. And he can fire everybody in the company, from the chairman on down, simply by spending his money somewhere else.
—SAM WALTON, founder, Wal-Mart Stores, Inc.

In 1986 I bought a brand new Lincoln Continental. When it was two years old someone asked, "How do you like your Lincoln?" I replied, "When it wears out, all I want is another one just like it." I kept it for six years and traded it in 1992. On the day I traded it in, I felt it was the finest car I had ever owned.

So when I traded my Lincoln in 1992, you might guess that I bought another Lincoln, right?

Wrong. I bought a Cadillac Seville STS the very same week that General Motors announced that it had incurred record losses, was making massive layoffs, and closing numerous plants.

I liked the Cadillac very much, but I can't say that I felt it was definitely the most car for the money when I bought it. Neither did I get a terrific break on the price from the dealer; in fact, I thought the price was rather steep. Nor, finally, was my buying decision based on patriotism, altruism, or even masochism.

So, why did I buy a Cadillac? Because one of the local Cadillac dealers offered something that the local Lincoln dealer did not: a reputation for outstanding service.

You see, a few years ago the Sewell family opened a Cadillac-Chevrolet dealership in my hometown of New Orleans. And when it comes to service, Sewell is to dealerships what Nordstrom is to retailing and Disney is to theme parks. Their reputation for customer care and outstanding service is legendary. That's why I bought a Cadillac. If the dealership was Sewell Dodge-Chrysler, I would have bought a Chrysler. And if it was Sewell Lincoln-Mercury, I would be driving a Lincoln.

Everybody sells good cars today. The difference is service. Carl Sewell learned long ago that there's a whole lot of money in building a business that revolves around the customer—our first commandment of speed.

LOVE THE ONES YOU'RE WITH

Winning more business in less time means winning new customers faster and keeping them. While fancy sales pitches and high-powered advertising may initially help, that's not where the real action is. When it comes to customers, the best way to speed up your business is to take very special care of the customers you already have.

It's the satisfied customer who comes back to make more and greater purchases year after year. It's the satisfied customer who brings in their spouse, son, daughter, or friends to make a purchase. It's the satisfied customer who tells others about how great it is to do business with your company.

In short, it's the satisfied customer who builds your reputation. And nothing creates customers faster or keeps them longer than a great reputation. Success in business always begins and ends by taking very special care of those who are indispensable to the business—the customers.

Not long ago I saw the message on the next page posted in a

small business for all of its employees to see. You may want to photocopy and post it where you work.

As simple and obvious as that message is, paying attention to it could save a lot of companies and entire industries from financial ruin. The U.S. auto industry is an excellent example. For years, U.S. auto executives believed they worked for the stockholders. They worked hard to keep quarterly profits and dividends high in order to make their stock attractive. Little attention was paid to producing quality products and investing for the long haul.

Rank-and-file workers believed that they worked for the union. Their agenda was to do the minimum amount of work required to hold their jobs and demand greater pay and benefits.

The dealers' agenda was to manipulate the customer into paying as much as possible for a new car, and frequently offering subpar service. Do you know anybody who enjoys new car shopping? Do you know any car owner who doesn't have a horror story about dealership service? For most car owners "dealership service" is like "jumbo shrimp": an oxymoron.

Everyone focused on their own agenda but almost no one focused on the customer. And customers vote with their feet—and their dollars.

Carl Sewell calculates the lifetime value of an automobile customer at $332,000 and treats each one that way. When a successful grocer I know sees an angry customer walk out the door of his store, he thinks, "There goes $50,000." His thinking is that if a customer buys $100 worth of groceries once a week for ten years, it adds up to well over $50,000. It costs five to six times more to win a new customer than it does to keep one. Yet loyal customers are on average worth ten times the price of a single purchase. How much revenue does a lifetime or a ten-year customer generate where you work? It's probably much more than you think.

But there is a lot more at stake than simply increasing revenue.

A BUSINESS PHILOSOPHY

In order to be successful, we have to sell our goods at a profit and satisfy our customers.

If we satisfy our customers but fail to make a profit, we will soon be out of business.

If we make a profit without satisfying our customers, we will soon be out of customers.

The secret of doing both lies in the one word *service*. Service means doing something so valuable for the customer that he is glad to pay a price that allows us to make a profit.

While losing customers is very costly, it turns out that keeping customers over time is one of the most profitable things a business can do. In the September-October 1990 issue of *Harvard Business Review*, Frederick E. Reichheld and W. Earl Sasser, Jr., wrote, "As a customer's relationship with the company lengthens, profits rise. And not just a little. Companies can boost profits by almost 100% by retaining just 5% more of their customers."

Keeping customers is highly profitable for several reasons. First, it costs about one fifth as much to keep a satisfied customer as it does to win a new one. And the cost per year of servicing a customer decreases for every additional year you keep him.

Second, customers buy more from you for each year that they stay with you. Once again, let's use an auto dealership as an example. A young couple just starting out may buy an economy car. Several years later, with small children, they may trade in the economy car or supplement it with a station wagon, van, or family-size sedan. As time goes by, they may bring in one or more of their children to buy a car, while still purchasing a car or two for themselves every several years. Finally, when the children are grown and they have more discretionary income, the couple may opt for one or more premium cars that are highly profitable.

Third, the potential profit from referrals and good word-of-mouth testimonials from satisfied customers is incalculable but enormous. A few years ago, I was interviewed on "Nation's Business Today," an early-morning business news program that aired weekday mornings on ESPN. During the interview, the hostess told of a friend who went shopping for shoes at a department store in a suburban Washington, D.C., mall. The salesperson noticed that one of the customer's feet was slightly larger than the other. So she took one shoe from one box and another shoe from another box to insure the customer a perfect fit. She charged the customer for only one pair of shoes, and several days later the customer received a hand-written note from the salesperson thanking her for her business. After the hostess told the story I asked, "Was that a Nordstrom store?" It was.

I don't remember what I said on the air, but after the interview I realized the impact of what had happened. For the wholesale price of one pair of shoes, Nordstrom had gotten an unsolicited, bona fide, free testimonial on national cable television from two people who weren't even customers! Do you think Madison Avenue can match that for cost-effective advertising? No way.

Finally, satisfied customers and satisfied employees thrive off of each other. As customer satisfaction increases, employee morale tends to rise. Higher employee morale means less turnover, lower training costs, and fewer mistakes from inexperienced workers. And fewer mistakes creates even more customer satisfaction, which, in turn, creates even greater employee satisfaction. The positive spiral goes onward and upward.

Conversely, in addition to being bad for business, dissatisfied customers tend to create dissatisfied employees and vice versa. Consequently, where customers are dissatisfied, you are likely to find high levels of employee stress, absenteeism and turnover, as well as layoffs. In this case, the negative spiral goes backward and downward.

WHAT IT TAKES IS WHATEVER IT TAKES

Duane Rath is Chairman of Rath Manufacturing Co. The company makes stainless-steel tubing for the food-processing and pharmaceutical industries and is a model of an excellent, efficiently run small business. When he was only seven years old, Rath learned the value of taking special care of the customer.

Young Duane was dragging a red wagon door-to-door in rural Sac City, Iowa, selling the likes of pancake mix and vanilla extract. In the town was an elderly school teacher who never answered her door when Duane came calling. But one day she came out and told Duane that if he would get her cat down from the tree she would buy some pancake mix. Duane promptly crawled up the tree, got the cat, and delivered it safely to the woman's waiting arms. According to Rath, "She couldn't possibly have eaten all the pancake mix I sold her." Never again would he underestimate the importance of going the extra mile for the customer.

That heartwarming anecdote makes a very important point:

Give customers whatever they want, how they want it, when they want it, wherever they want it. Do whatever it takes to create happy, delighted, satisfied customers.

Once again, another simple, obvious idea. But what is so simple in concept is often overlooked in execution. Here are three actual examples of what I mean:

Jim Hannah dialed a toll-free 800 number to place an order for software. The call was answered, "John Doe, may I help you?"
"Yes, I'd like to order Beagle Brothers 'Time-Out Quickspell.' "
"Uh . . . could you call us back in about ten minutes? We're in the middle of a very important sales meeting."
Dumfounded that a sales meeting was more important than making a sale, Jim placed his order elsewhere.

New Orleans bank customer: "Excuse me. I would like to make a deposit to my account, but I left my deposit slips at home."
Bank Employee: "I'm sorry, but I can't help you. I work in customer service."
The bank has since fallen on hard times and been taken over.

Mark Sanborn to an airline employee supervisor: "I just waited in two lines for over an hour and no one has been able to give me the

information that I need for my connecting flight. I just want you to
know that I'm never going to fly on your airline again."

Supervisor: "We will miss you terribly."

In case you're wondering, it was Eastern Airlines.

Remember them?

Sometimes it seems as if businesses actually make a conscious
effort to run off their customers. The Lincoln dealership where I
brought my Continental to be serviced was a classic example. I
know that there are numerous, high-quality, excellent Lincoln
dealerships with great reputations for service. This dealership
isn't one of them, although it once was.

On two separate occasions I tried to buy a car from them to no
avail. The first time was in 1986. The salesman asked me if I
wanted to trade in my current model or just buy the Lincoln. I
asked him to give me a price both ways and I'd make a decision.
He refused. I asked if they would be willing to order a car from the
factory for me with the color and options I wanted. The salesman
replied that the boss didn't like to order cars. I bought my car from
a dealer on the other side of town.

The dealership did excellent repair, maintenance, and body
work, but their style in handling the customer was early Nean-
derthal. On numerous occasions when I brought the car in for
service I was told, "Call us next week and make an appointment,"
by a service writer reminiscent of Saddam Hussein. When customers drive into their service area, the first thing they see is a
giant white banner with large red letters hanging from the ceiling
that reads NO CUSTOMERS ALLOWED IN WORK AREA. How's that
for rolling out the red carpet? In other words, "Look, all you idiots
who pay the bills, keep out so we can get some work done."

When I pointed out the sign to one of the owners he told me it
was necessary for the customers' safety. If that's the case, how

about a sign that reads, "Customers, we appreciate your business but value your safety and well-being most of all. For this reason, we request that you please not enter the work area." It may seem like a little thing. But when it comes to service, little things don't mean a lot. They mean everything.

In 1991, I tried once again to buy a car from the same dealership. When the salesman started playing the same old games, I told him, "I tried to buy a car here five years ago but got the runaround and bought one across town. If you want to sell me a car, I will choose the model, color, interior, and options that I want. And I also want the services of a loaner car when I bring my car in to be serviced. If I can't get what I want from you, I'm going to buy a Cadillac from Sewell, who will provide me with these services. Now, what's it going to be?"

The salesman immediately summoned one of the owners, who came out, gave me a slick smile and said, "Michael, we really value your business and want to sell you a new Lincoln." I replied, "Do you want to sell a car or create a customer?" He answered, "Both." But as for loaner cars, they had tried it, and it didn't work for them. He offered to guarantee me rental-car reimbursement when I brought my car in for service. I explained that wasn't a satisfactory arrangement for me because securing a rental car is too time-consuming.

It was then that I realized they weren't selling what I wanted to buy. I was trying to buy hassle-free transportation. They were trying to sell me a car.

The following day I went to Sewell Cadillac, where I met Joe Raymond, a delightful salesman who has been selling Cadillacs for almost 30 years. He patiently let me test-drive all the '91 models, but nothing really got me excited. But instead of trying to talk up one of the current models, Joe looked at my Lincoln and said, "You really don't need a new car yet and the all-new Seville is coming out in '92. Let's stay in touch. It may be just the car for you." A few months later he sent me a copy of *Car and Driver* with rave reviews of the Seville.

In February 1992 I had a birthday coming up and decided to treat myself to a new car. I test-drove the Seville STS and decided that was what I wanted. But by that time the car was a smash hit, winning numerous "car of the year" awards, and was in very short supply. Sewell didn't have any in stock, and Joe said it might take up to 60 days to order one with the color and options I wanted from the factory. I was perfectly willing to wait.

The following Monday, Joe called. They had located an STS just like I wanted at a dealership almost 500 miles away. Did I want it? You bet.

We closed the deal on Monday afternoon. They immediately dispatched a driver with a trailer, who drove all night to pick up the car. He loaded the STS early Tuesday morning and arrived back in New Orleans Tuesday afternoon. On Wednesday afternoon I picked up the car—the day before my birthday. Sewell Cadillac got me the car I wanted, the way I wanted it, when I wanted it. They went the extra mile for the customer. Bravo!

HOW TO STAY FOCUSED ON THE CUSTOMER

It's been said that the only people who aren't in the service business are blood donors. The rest of us are ultimately selling service in some form to an ultimate customer who makes our livelihood possible. And those who serve best tend to profit most and enjoy greater job security and satisfaction. (I would argue that even blood donors are in the service business.)

Staying focused on the customer is an idea that is much easier said than done. Make no mistake about it. Giving customers what they want, how they want it, whenever they want it, the way they want it is difficult. Very difficult. But like it or not, that's where the money is. Business is not rocket science. It's about two things: money and customers. And without the customers there's no money and no business. It's that simple.

The following are six key ideas to help you keep your eyes, your team, and/or your business focused on the customer.

1. Treat Your Customers Like Lifetime Partners

Treating customers like partners is one of the best things you can do for your business and your customers. A lifetime partner isn't someone you manipulate into buying what you have in stock. He's someone you listen to so you can help him get what he wants by doing business with you. He isn't someone whose problems and special requests are treated lightly. You want him to know that *nobody* is going to take better care of him than you will. Once the customer knows this, he won't even consider taking his business anywhere else. You become his friend, someone he knows he can depend on, and buying from you becomes a habit. Best of all, by referring new customers to you, he acts as your advertising agency and goodwill ambassador all rolled into one. And he pays you! Such a deal!

2. Look at Your Business Through Your Customers' Eyes

Virtually every successful business and business person that I know of has great customer empathy. The key to success in business lies in knowing what's going on inside your customers' hearts and minds. What do they want? Where's the pain? How can you make them glad to be your customer? What do they pay for? How do you create value for them?

Customer empathy comes naturally for some, such as Phyllis Grann, Chairman and CEO of The Putnam Berkley Group, Inc. When it comes to the high-risk business of picking fiction bestsellers, nobody does it better. As an avid fiction reader, she literally lives her market, and her tastes and preferences are very much attuned to what the readers will buy.

But for most of us, customer empathy comes from staying close to our customers, asking questions, and keeping our eyes and ears open. Managers at TGI Friday's Restaurants periodically sit at every chair and table in the bar and restaurant and look at it through the customer's eyes. Is the place clean? Are the employees friendly? Is the service prompt and the food delicious? *Reader's Digest* makes regular mailings to over 50 million U.S. households. A file is kept on each subscriber to track customer purchases and preferences. According to Chairman George Grune, "It tells us their likes and dislikes. Our relationship with the reader is the key to the success of this company."

Tony Richards, Vice President of Education and Training for the D.C. Credit Union League, has a great way of reminding employees to look at themselves through the customer's eyes. He passes out a simple white card the size of a business card that asks: WHAT IS YOUR IMAGE RIGHT NOW? He asks employees to put the card by their telephones or teller windows where they can readily see it. Whenever things get stressful and they think they are about to lose their cool with a customer or colleague, Tony asks employees to look at the card and consider the question before reacting. He also carries the cards with him and passes them out when he is a customer and gets exceptional or poor service.

3. What Results Do I Produce in My Job and How Do They Benefit the Customer?

Answer that question in as few words as possible. Every job, every department, and every work team must directly or indirectly contribute to winning and keeping customers or it needs to be eliminated.

This doesn't mean that your job needs to include customer contact to be vital. A cook in a restaurant may never meet a customer, but he has a major influence on the customer's dining experience. A janitorial team cleaning corporate offices after hours may never see a customer or a regular employee. But it benefits the customer by creating a better work environment for customers to visit or for others to work in as they serve the customer. A financial-records department contributes by keeping track of payroll, billing, and numerous financial transactions that make it possible for the business and its people to continue serving the customer. No matter what your job is, you need to understand its role in creating and keeping customers. Why? Because the customer signs everybody's paycheck.

If you're an owner or manager, make answering the above question a required exercise for everyone—starting with you. In addition to focusing your job on the customer, there's another wonderful payoff. When you start evaluating all the activities of your job in terms of their impact on the customer, all the unnecessary work that wastes your time becomes very apparent, and you can stop doing it.

4. Sales and Service Are Everybody's Job

Customer-focused businesses realize that you don't win and keep customers with a cracker-jack sales force and front-line people with nice smiles. It takes a lot more than that.

Federal Express believes that every one of their employees must be sales oriented and that every manager must be an outstanding salesperson. Every officer in the company is assigned to a sales district, where he spends a portion of each quarter working with salespeople and visiting customers. This keeps the management customer-focused and helps Federal Express develop services tailored to customer needs. If you ask, "How many people at Federal Express are in sales?" they answer, "All of them."

Similarly, customer service is not a department. It's an attitude. There's no room for "It's not my department" in a world where customers have so many choices. At the Nightingale-Conant Corporation in Chicago, everyone wears a T-shirt or sweatshirt (depending on the season) to work on Fridays. Printed on every shirt is the following message: CUSTOMER SERVICE IS MY JOB.

5. Everybody Is Somebody's Customer

Another way to stay focused on the customer is to use the concept of the internal customer. Satisfying the ultimate customer requires us to provide service to others inside the business as well. For example, in a restaurant, the cook's internal customer is the waiter. It's his job to provide the waiter with prompt service by cooking delicious meals ordered by the customer to the customer's liking.

Your main internal customer is usually the person who receives the output of your work. The idea is to create a chain of customers whose ultimate purpose is to satisfy the external customer. Or, to put it another way: *If you aren't directly serving the customer, your job is to serve someone who is.*

One obvious implication of this is that management's main internal customers are those who produce the goods and services for the external customer. This idea was best illustrated to me by a Senior Vice President of a large corporation. Instead of "Senior Vice President," the title printed on his business card read: "Helper."

6. Remember, It's the Little Things

Great service isn't the product of doing anything a thousand percent better. It comes from doing thousands of things one percent better. It's the follow-up phone call, the sincere compliment, the personal thank-you note, the quick resolution of a customer's complaint, and doing something special for the customer that lets him know he's number one. It's a day-in, day-out, on-going, never-ending pursuit. But it's the sum total of the little things that have such a huge impact on the bottom line.

One of the things I enjoy most is hearing from people who have read my books, listened to my tapes, or heard me speak and share their experiences and ideas with me. Jim Hannah's experience ordering software and Tony Richards' card are two examples, and I will share many more with you in the following chapters. I especially enjoyed the following letter because I think it illustrates how little things make the big difference. The letter is from Miriam Piccinini of Roxbury, Connecticut, who writes:

I also have an experience to share with you that involves keeping customers. About eight years ago my family and I traveled to Washington, D.C., to attend a function. We stayed at a Marriott Hotel and enjoyed our stay very much. As we were leaving, I picked up the comment card from our room, filled it out, and turned it in— as something to do—never expecting anything to come of it. Imagine my surprise when weeks later a letter arrived at my house from J. W. Marriott, Jr., saying he was grateful for my comments, was glad I enjoyed my stay, and hoped I would stay with Marriott again soon. (The now-president of one of the world's largest hotel companies writing to thank one 14-year-old girl for her comments!) Of course, now when I travel I never stay at any other hotel than a Marriott and am considering a future management career with them.

Another great testimonial, another lifetime customer, and another company that's doing a lot more business in turbulent times. For over 20 years the Marriott Corporation's growth rate has averaged a phenomenal 20 percent per year.

2 Get in Step With the Future

Every time I figure out where it's at, somebody moves it.
—ZIGGY

"The prize goes to the person who sees the future the quickest." That's the gospel according to William Stiritz, Chairman of Ralston Purina Co. If the "prize" is success in a rapidly changing world, then the key to your future is being among the first to discover and satisfy your customers' unmet wants. But proceed with caution.

A few years ago I was one of two people invited to speak to a group of corporate executives. The other invited speaker was Faith Popcorn, author of *The Popcorn Report* and world famous trend forecaster to major corporations. The original plan was for Ms. Popcorn to speak, followed by yours truly. But her flight was delayed, and they asked me to speak first. So I began my talk by saying, "You were originally scheduled to hear a futurist at this time. Unfortunately, she isn't able to be here because of an unforeseen happening." In today's fast-moving, turbulent world even futurists get surprised.

Don't misunderstand me. I'm a great believer in trend watching and trend forecasters. In the midst of a storm it's wise to have all the weather instruments you can muster. What I would caution you against is taking any observation, prediction, or trend as absolute gospel for the future, including the ones you are about to read in this chapter. Use them as broad indicators to make sure you are riding the horse in the direction the horse is going. But be advised that today's horse is an untamed stallion, and the ride is going to be full of surprises.

The best sources of advice for future opportunities are your own customers and those who you want to become your customers. Ask, listen, and learn from them—frequently. Then decide what it's going to take to make them love doing business with you, and do it. If what they tell you they want is counter to a trend, forget the trend and give the customers what they want. The trend may not apply in your industry or to your customers.

Most of us are *reactive* by nature. We believe "If it ain't broke, don't fix it"—a good rule-of-thumb for non-turbulent times and situations. But in today's business world, if it ain't broke, it will be soon. If you wait for things to break and then react, you may be too late and miss a golden opportunity.

The purpose of this chapter is to help you be *proactive*, or to paraphrase the Panasonic slogan, "Just slightly ahead of your time." That's where the money is. The pioneers too far out in front get the arrows and those arriving late get the leftovers. But those who correctly anticipate the future and get there ahead of the crowd are the winners.

PUTTING CHANGE IN PERSPECTIVE

Before going into specific aspects of how the business world is changing, let's back off and look at the big picture. We all view the world through our own unique pair of binoculars that magnify our immediate world and its problems—the trees—but which blind us to the scope and direction of change—the forest. So let's turn your binoculars around and look at the world through the opposite end, which gives you a much broader overview. With two views of the world, the big picture and your regular, closeup view, you're better equipped to anticipate and capitalize on future changes.

The Shrinking of Time and Space

As I wrote at the outset, all of this massive, unpredictable change is being caused by technology. The late Marshall McLuhan gave us a very useful framework for understanding the impact of technology when he taught us to think of inventions as extensions of ourselves.

Just as advancements in transportation are extensions of our feet and labor-saving tools and machines are extensions of our muscles, media (print, radio, fax, television, telephone, satellites) are extensions of our eyes and ears and our ability to communicate. Until the nineteenth century, people only knew what was happening at the moment in their immediate surroundings. Today we are capable of knowing instantaneously what is happening anywhere in the world. The Battle of New Orleans in 1814 was fought after the peace treaty had been signed and the war was over. But in 1991 we sat in homes and offices throughout the world and witnessed the Persian Gulf War live. We've come a long way.

But the technological breakthrough that has created the most change to date is the electronic computer, and it's turning the world upside down. It is accelerating rapid changes in transportation, labor, communication, and virtually every facet of our lives. Why? Because while all the other breakthroughs are extensions of our bodies, the computer is the first extension of our minds.

With computers we have brilliant idiots to do some of our thinking for us. Each one has an enormous memory with perfect, instantaneous recall capability. They perform arithmetic calculations flawlessly at light speed. But best of all, we can teach them to make decisions for us. And they're making more and more of them with every passing day.

If you think you don't own a computer, guess again. If you own a telephone with a memory or instant redial function, you own a computer. If you own a microwave oven, television, programmable thermostat, or any number of common household appliances, chances are you own a computer. There is more computer technology in today's average automobile than in the Apollo spacecraft that went to the moon in 1969.

Mix computer technology with other advances and you create a whole new world. The modern media represents the marriage of the computer with telephone, print, radio, fax, television, and satellite technologies.

Marry machines with computers and you get robots doing what was blue-collar work. Put computers to work on Wall Street and you get programmed trading. Put computers to work in the telephone companies or company switchboards and you find them performing jobs once held by operators. Put them to work in management and you find them analyzing data and making routine decisions once made by middle management.

The arrival of the computer ended the industrial age and ushered in the information age. Today most of us earn our livelihood producing information or providing services for each other. While manufacturing is still important, the jobs simply aren't going to be there in any great number. Just as technology slashed the number of farmers, it is reducing the number of manufacturing employees as robots and computers do more of the work.

And blue-collar workers aren't the only ones being displaced. It's happening in the clerical white-collar, and middle-management ranks too. In earlier times, people were cheap and technology was expensive. Today the reverse is true. And with each passing year, technology will become less expensive, more competent, and do more of the work formerly done by people.

Biotechnology is the latest arrival. It's in its infancy and promises to have the greatest impact of all. Imagine being able to choose the height, hair and eye color, sex, IQ, and numerous other characteristics of your children. Imagine being able to lengthen the human life span indefinitely, or to prevent and cure previously incurable diseases through genetic alteration. Imagine being able to grow or replace an arm, leg, or internal organ when your current ones wear out. Those are just a few possibilities of the biotech era, and the implications are staggering. For the first time in history, humans will have the potential to play God. Human values will face serious tests in the twenty-first century.

Other Major Trends

Here, in brief, are some other major trends and changes that are shaping our work and our lives. Notice that all of these are direct or indirect consequences of technology.

• *We are scared*. Crime, drugs, nuclear power, a polluted environment, terrorists, AIDS, escalating health-care costs, distrust of our leaders, and job insecurity are causing us to see the world as a very unsafe place. As a result, more of us are looking for refuge and centering our lives around our homes. Sales of home-security systems, hand guns, water and air filters, expensive kitchens, lavish bath and bedrooms, luxury entertainment centers, and home-office equipment are all rising.

• *Gray power*. Every major industrialized nation is facing an aging population. Advances in health care have lengthened life spans while advances in family planning have trimmed birth rates. The average American's life span in 1900 was 45 for men and 47 for women. Today it's approaching 80 and rising. There are more U. S. citizens over 65 than the entire population of Canada. The AARP membership represents over 20 percent of American voters and is sure to increase with each passing year.

- *The baby boomers*. Born after the big war and before the pill, there are 76 million of them in the United States. Demographically speaking, they are *the* market. Their numbers are so immense that they will continue to dictate taste, preferences, and where and how most of the dollars are spent. In 1996, the oldest boomers will be 50.

- *A widening gap between the rich and the poor*. The blue-collar worker faces a shrinking market for his services. Much the same is true for clerical workers and managers who perform routine work in bureaucracies. Differences between the haves and have-nots will be determined largely by education. The future looks bright for the knowledge worker and even brighter for the knowledge entrepreneur.

- *Diversity*. Women, Blacks, Hispanics, and Asians are increasing as a percentage of the labor force, giving them more clout at work and more buying power in the market place. Getting people with such differing values and backgrounds to work as a team and appealing to them as customers in the market are major challenges for business.

- *Multi-option lifestyles*. The traditional nuclear family, where the husband does the bread-winning and the wife manages the home, is no longer the norm. Today you can choose from an endless combination of work/family lifestyles.

- *Choices, choices, choices*. These, more than any other reason, are why life is so different and sometimes so overwhelming today. Look at products, services, careers, lifestyles, or whatever over the past 20 years and one thing becomes very obvious: The number of choices available to you in almost every category has exploded. In 1970 I had the choice of watching three network television stations and two independents. In 1980, thanks to cable television, my number of viewing choices was increased to 36. In the 1990s a satellite dish gives me literally hundreds of viewing choices. Deciding what to watch is like trying to choose a wall paper pattern: too many choices!

BUSINESS LESSONS FROM THE BIG PICTURE

Needless to say, the major changes and trends are creating sweeping changes in the world of business. Now let's turn your binoculars back around, look at how these changes are affecting business, and consider how you can capitalize on them.

Let the Seller Beware

Forget "Caveat emptor" or "Let the buyer beware." The new rule is "Let the seller beware." Todays customers are much better informed and have an ever-increasing number of places to spend their money. If they have the slightest doubt about your credibility, or feel they can get a better deal elsewhere, they are more than happy to take their business down the street, or to the other side of the world. Lawyers in London are faxing their typing to Taiwan because it's cheaper.

Competition in almost every business is mushrooming. In twenty years the number of companies competing with IBM exploded from 20 to over 5,000. Between 1971 and 1991, the number of semiconductor companies jumped from 90 to over 300. The introduction of digital technology is blurring the lines between four giant industries. The computer, consumer electronics, communications, and entertainment businesses suddenly find themselves in competition with each other. Suddenly it seems like everybody is in everybody else's business.

When your business faces unpredictable change and enormous

competition you have no choice but to build the business around the customer. But deciding to focus on the customer means making enormous changes in the way most businesses operate. You don't just hang out a banner proclaiming, "The Customer Is Always Right" and send everyone to smile-training classes. There's much more to it than that. Here are some of the major changes involved:

• *The customer becomes a partner and an integral part of your business.* He is no longer someone who just buys what your company happens to produce and/or sell. Both parties work together in concert to produce a mutually beneficial, long-term relationship.

• *Professional salespeople with good listening skills and great product knowledge are imperative.* Traditional, manipulative, Willy Loman–type sales tactics are out. It's the salesperson's job to close the sale and a whole lot more. In the customer-focused business, great selling and great service are one and the same. Customers are too hard to win and too valuable to lose.

• *There is less mass marketing and more niche and micromarketing.* The population has become so diverse and so splintered that reaching buyers through mass advertising and marketing can be very wasteful.

For example, let's consider television advertising. There was a time when a business could place a spot on local television and be assured of reaching a sizable audience of potential buyers. Today, because of cable television, viewers have more choices, and a smaller percentage of viewers see the spot. Additionally, there's the remote-control freak (I'm one of them) who scans the channels during commercials. Then on top of that, there's the viewer who tapes the show and fast-forwards their VCR through the commercials. In this case, technology makes it harder to reach the buyer.

But a customer-focused business takes a different approach to marketing. Traditional marketing focuses on getting the customer to buy what we sell. Customer-focused marketing concentrates on selling what the customer wants to buy. Much less effort is placed on persuading everyone in the market to buy. Instead, we target a specific segment or niche of the market, and learn as much as we can about who they are and how we can serve them. Once again, the ultimate goal isn't just to make a sale but to get the customer married to the business.

Modern technology makes it possible to learn an incredible amount about customer preferences very quickly. Even in a large, mass-goods business like snack foods, there are tremendous micromarketing possibilities. Frito-Lay works closely with its retail outlets as computerized check-out scanners provide an instant analysis of what products and how many are moving off the shelves. All of Frito-Lay's 10,000 salespeople carry hand-held computers that feed sales information daily to a central computer in Plano, Texas. To quote one sales rep, "In 1980 I could have told you how Doritos are selling west of the Mississippi. Today I can tell you how they're selling not only in California but also in Orange County, in the town of Irvine, in the local Von's, in the special promotion at the end of aisle four, on Thursday."

All of this information makes it possible to sell more customers exactly what they want, when they want, and where they want it. And with the guess work taken out of selling, the wasteful expense of producing, packaging, and shipping unsold snacks is greatly reduced. Not surprisingly, the Frito-Lay division of PepsiCo is one of the world's most profitable businesses with operating margins of over 20 percent.

• *There is less mass production and more emphasis on producing customized goods and services.* The old Henry Ford paradigm of selling the customer a car in any color he wants as long as it's black is about the worst axiom for the future that I can think of. The more we tailor our products and services to each customer's liking, the more value each customer perceives and the greater are the chances of keeping him. Customization is the future.

For example, McGraw-Hill, Eastman Kodak, and R. R. Donnelley & Sons have teamed up and are now publishing customized text books for individual professors and their classes. As an alternative to the standard textbook, each professor can design his own text. Customized texts include items such as chapters from different books, study-guide exercises, recent articles, case studies, the professor's own writings, and the course syllabus. All of this is then assembled, in the order the professor wants, printed (with the name of the university, the professor, and the course on the cover), and bound and shipped within a matter of days.

I spoke with a professor who is teaching from his own customized text and he is delighted. He reports that the customized text cost the students less and that it took only a matter of days, rather than weeks, to get them.

Capitalize on Customer Buying Trends

A fundamental question that every business needs to ask itself frequently is, "Are we really selling what the customer wants to buy?" Since I don't know what business you're in or who your customers are, I can't answer the question for you. But I can help you get a more accurate answer.

The following are five major, evolving trends that show no

indication of fading. Examine your current and potential products/ services in light of each trend.

1. Customers value time more than money. "So much to do, so little time" describes the dilemma of most people today. The average American today is working 140 hours more per year than 20 years ago. All those predictions of the four-day work week and the promise of increased leisure time have not materialized. Laptop computers, voice mail, cellular phones, fax machines, beepers, and all those convenient "time-saving" devices have us working longer hours. Instead of leaving the job at the office, more people are taking their jobs home, in the car, on the plane, on vacation, or wherever they go.

While work hours have increased, leisure hours have declined. During the eighties, paid time off for vacations, sick leave, personal days, and holidays declined 15 percent. Add the time pressures of the two-career couple with all those choices available, and you have too many people trying to do too much. People are so starved for time that most Americans would happily trade away part of their paycheck for an extra day off each week.

The two main lessons of this trend are:

- If you want to make money, save the customer time.
- If you want to lose money, make the customer wait.

Customer convenience is the currency of the present and future. Everything from home-delivery services, to ready-made meals, to gadgets like the VCR Plus, which simplifies programming your video cassette recorder, are products and services in step with the future.

2. *This is the age of Value marketing.* Simply put, we have gone from the Gucci decade to the Wal-Mart decade. During the eighties, we got high on conspicuous consumption. Customers, businesses, and the government got drunk on overspending and are feeling the hangover in the nineties. Buying patterns have become more conservative and show little indication of returning to the extravagances of the eighties.

What customers are willing to pay for is *value*—the greatest combination of quality and service (as seen through the customer's eyes) at the lowest possible price. This is one key reason why Wal-Mart, Home Depot, Office Depot, Taco Bell, Southwest Airlines, and the like are profiting so handsomely. They begin by offering the customer the best possible price and add value to the package. You can create value any number of ways, including:

- Offering only reliable products.
- Exceeding the customer's expectation by going the extra mile, or throwing in something extra.
- Offering no-risk shopping with a no-questions-asked, money-back guarantee.
- Providing free pickup and delivery.
- Giving the customer detailed information on how to get the most from your products/services.
- Being readily available to help customers whenever they have a problem.

Saving the customer time, customizing products, and building a special relationship with the customer are all value-building activities. Do it. It's crucial. As General Electric Chairman Jack Welch put it, "If you can't sell a top-quality product at the world's lowest price, you're going to be cut of the game."

3. Follow the boomers. Actually the baby boomers aren't a trend. They're a demographic reality. The oldest were born in 1946 and the youngest in 1964. If you want to know where most of the money is, follow the boomers. They are the largest age group and trendsetters of the population. And they are getting richer. The oldest boomers are now in the peak-earning years of 45–55. Furthermore, in the next quarter century, boomers will inherit a total of over $6 trillion from their parents.

Although older and more conservative, boomers have their own unique way of thinking and their own set of values. Remember, these are the people who gave us Woodstock, free love, pro-choice, quality-of-life, conspicuous consumption, feminism, save the planet, Hippies, Yippies, Yuppies, and Bellyuppies (Yuppies who went broke). As I see it, the greatest effects of the aging boomers will be in four areas.

First, maturity is going to become the greatest thing since sliced bread. Don't be surprised if a reverse ageism develops that discounts youth. "What could they possibly know? They haven't lived." Neighborhoods that ban children are already a reality in some retirement communities. In the sixties, the prevailing slogan was, "Never trust anyone over 30." Now we are being told that life begins at 40. Pretty soon we will hear "50 is nifty," to be followed by "60 is sexy," "70 is heavenly," and "the best of your life is the rest of your life." Businesses that reinforce those messages at the appropriate time will be loved and patronized by boomers.

Second, boomers will escalate the health-care, fitness, and wellness-related industries. The next 20 years will be the golden age of cosmetic surgery. The emphasis won't be on restoring youth but maintaining a mature, well-kept look. Any product or service that helps boomers to look and feel better about themselves, or to live happier, more active, lives will thrive.

Third, as more boomers become empty-nesters, their free time and discretionary incomes will rise. This will create a bonanza for recreational, retirement, entertainment, and financial services enterprises.

Fourth, and this is very important, remember that a lot of boomers are serious environmentalists. Being pro-environment is good business. Sebastian International, a successful maker of beauty-care products, credits its green image as the key reason company annual sales doubled to $100 million in five years. It dropped several top-selling hair dyes and sprays because they weren't "environmentally friendly." It began giving carpooling employees a free shampoo and became a big supporter of efforts to save the Amazon rain forest. According to John Cusenza, Sebastian's founder and president, "This is the way we see the consumer moving. . . . They're going to buy based on what the company stands for."

Don't allow your business to do *anything* that can be perceived as threatening or abusive to the planet or any creatures on it. Hopefully, you will do this because it's the right thing to do. Pragmatically, you better do it or risk facing a mass exodus of customers and more headaches than you could ever imagine.

4. Information is money. Unless you have been asleep for the past decade, you know that we are currently living in the information age. It started in the fifties with the advent of the computer. But most of us didn't begin to fathom the economic upheaval it would create until the eighties. In the industrial age, capital and energy were keys to creating wealth. But in the information age, creating, assembling, selling, and distributing useful knowledge and delivering service are the keys to wealth creation.

For example, Bill Gates, founder of Microsoft Corporation, has become a young billionaire by creating and selling computer software. Microsoft isn't creating and selling computers. They are creating and selling information that enables us to make better use of the computer. A blank floppy disc retails for about a dollar. Put a word-processing, spread-sheet or data-base program on the disc and its market value jumps to hundreds of dollars.

This book would be virtually worthless if the pages were blank. The information printed on the pages creates the value.

Other examples abound. *TV Guide* was purchased in 1987 for over $2 billion, an amount that exceeded the market value of either the CBS, ABC, or NBC television networks at that time.

The *Official Airlines Guide* (OAG) consolidates and publishes monthly flight schedules of all the airlines. It then sells subscriptions to passengers who fly frequently or to anyone who needs this information at their fingertips. In 1988, it sold for $750 million, which was three times what TWA paid for Ozark Airlines, almost triple the value of the Eastern Shuttle, and slightly less than the market value of U.S. Air.

Quotron is a service that provides security prices information to stock brokers. It was purchased in 1988 by Citicorp for $628 million, more than the selling price of Paine-Webber or Smith-Barney in the late eighties.

In today's and tomorrow's world, it is possible to make more money from selling information and service related to the product than from selling the product. So if you want to revitalize your business or start a new one, consider supplementing an existing product with information and service. General Motors makes more profit from financing cars than it does from manufacturing and selling them.

5. *Beware the shrinking middle market.* There was a time when a business thrived by appealing to the mainstream of customers known as the middle class. It's getting harder and harder to survive in the middle market because the middle class is shrinking

and the number of customers at either end is growing. There are a lot more single-person and two-career households with very healthy incomes. At the same time, there are a lot more single-parent households with very little income. Knowledge workers are doing very well in the new economy. At the same time, an increasing number of clerical, middle-management, and blue-collar workers are finding themselves out of work and facing a bleak future.

As a result, companies that follow a mainstream strategy are losing market share. Sealtest ice cream, a mainstream brand, is struggling, while upscale "super premium" ice creams and grocers who own bargain labels are selling well. Wal-Mart with everyday minimum pricing and Nordstrom with incredible service are thriving. Traditional mainstream retailers such as Sears, J. C. Penney, and Macy's have suffered, and others have been driven totally out of business. Business is locking up at five-star hotels and cheap lodging chains, while traditional, mainstream chains such as Holiday Inn and Ramada Inn have been hurt.

There's little or no future in creating products and services that everyone likes a little. Either be the cheapest or the absolute best in your market and you'll find a ready and willing number of customers. Follow a value-marketing strategy and you will attract customers from both ends *and* the middle.

Think of Yourself as in Business for Yourself

Unpredictable change coupled with increased competition is forcing businesses to have fewer long-term employees. While you may find that an unpleasant fact, it's the shape of things to come.

Additionally, globalization is creating intense competition for all types of jobs. Assembly-line jobs aren't the only ones being exported. Today many professional, technical, and service jobs are easily moved to wherever they can be performed at the cheapest price. A number of U.S. computer companies are hiring Indian software writers who do excellent work for an average annual salary of $3,000. In Ireland, office workers process medical insurance claims for U.S. insurance companies. U.S. companies are hiring an increasing number of foreign engineers each year. Some work in their native land while others are imported. One can only imagine what the job competition will be like when a billion well-trained Chinese along with people from the former Soviet bloc enter the global market.

The rule for success in the future is: *Take charge of your own career and think of yourself as a one-person business.* Unless you are self-employed, your employer is your customer. They are buying your services for a specified or indefinite period, for an amount equal to your pay plus benefits. In return, you must provide quality service to your employer that is worth more to them than your compensation. And the amount of money your one-person business commands in the market place will depend on three factors:

- what you do;
- how well you do it;
- how difficult it is to replace you.

In his audio-cassette program "Lead the Field," the late Earl Nightingale tells a story from the Great Depression that many of us can learn and profit from. As you probably know, or may remember, the depression was a time of massive unemployment, bread lines, soup kitchens, and people clamoring, "I'll do anything if someone will just give me a job." Yet Earl had a friend who, at the bottom of the depression, discovered that he could go to work in almost any business he wanted. He discovered this after realizing that the businesses that were laying off people were just as anxious to succeed as the people who were looking for jobs. They too were worried about going broke and being out of work.

So here's what Earl's friend did. Instead of standing in long employment lines, filling out application forms, and mailing resumes, he picked out a company or industry where he wanted to work. Then he devoted a month to learning all he could about the business. He went to the library and read everything he could find about the industry. He talked and listened to people in the same line of work, probing for what they felt the problems were and what was wrong. Then he sat down and generated some ideas that he thought could help the business.

When he was ready, he called on the business where he wanted to work. But instead of asking for a job, he said to the boss, "I believe I know of several ways in which your business can be greatly increased, and I'd like to talk to you about them." He was a one-person business selling the one thing his customer wanted to buy. While others asked for a job, he offered ideas for growing the business. And he got the job.

Learn to Love Change and Be Ready for Anything

It's been said that we are all for change as long as it doesn't affect us. We all have an inherent tendency to cling to the familiar. For better or worse, it's what we know and where we feel comfortable and secure. But clinging to the rules and habits of yesterday can be as disastrous to our businesses and careers as the monkey trap is to the monkey.

In southern India, where they are considered a delicacy, monkeys are captured in an incredibly simple way. The monkey trap consists of a hollowed-out coconut, containing rice, chained to a stake. The hole in the coconut is large enough to accommodate the monkey's hand when he reaches in to grab the rice. However, once he grabs the rice he can't escape the trap. His fist is too wide to pass through the hole. Unless the monkey releases the rice and abandons his "sure meal," he is destined to become a meal. He isn't a victim of the trap. He is a victim of his own refusal to let go.

We all have a choice. We can let go of the past, welcome change, and take action to get in step with the future. Or we can cling to business as usual and let the future make monkeys of us.

3 Be an Innovator

There's a way to do it better—find it.
—THOMAS A. EDISON

You wake up one day and go to work thinking it's business as usual. But you soon learn that your company has been blindsided by the forces of change. A new competitor is offering products and services for half the price that make yours look stone-aged. "Impossible," you say? Well unless you work in a very stable industry that makes little-changing products, like toothpicks, matches, or manhole covers, it's a likely scenario for the future.

You can lessen the odds of such a horror story happening where you work by doing the following:

• *Continuously introduce new products and services that make your existing ones obsolete.*
• *Continuously work at improving the way things get done.* Continuous improvement through innovation (the application of new ideas) is the third commandment for winning more business in turbulent times. Offering the finest, most state-of-the-art products and services enables you to charge premium prices, increase market share, and make the business less vulnerable to the competition. And finding better, faster ways to get things done lowers costs, while increasing employee and customer satisfaction.

53

Innovation has always been a powerful, competitive weapon. But in a rapidly changing world, it's a survival skill. Virtually everything being done today will be done differently and better tomorrow. If you don't make your current products, services, and processes obsolete, you can be sure that a competitor will. In discussing their company philosophy, Home Depot founders Bernard Marcus and Arthur Blank have some excellent advice for today's businesses:

> If you don't make dust, you eat it. We have an ongoing commitment to running scared. . . . The whole focus of the company is to take today's standards and accept them for what they are but say we have to improve them for the future. Maintaining what we do today is just not going to cut it.

BARRIERS EVERYWHERE

While innovation is more important than ever, few companies are truly adept at the art of creating and implementing new ideas. Whether it's a new product or a new way to work smarter, all sorts of obstacles can magically appear to subvert a great idea. Here, in brief, are nine of the most common barriers to innovation. How many of these exist where you work?

1. Human Nature

Perhaps the most common barrier is the inherent human tendency to resist change. Implementing any new idea means giving up the status quo, with which we usually feel more comfortable and secure. Making a change requires us to abandon our comfort zone and replace the tried and true with the uncertain and unknown.

2. Money Myopia

Another potential barrier is the financial preoccupation with short-term earnings. A major innovation often means making a long-term commitment where the payoff may be years away. Those focused on the next quarter's earnings or the net present value of an idea often fail to see the long-term benefit. The result is that a great idea dies because "it didn't make the numbers." We can all be thankful that Thomas Edison didn't have an MBA.

3. "It's Not My Idea"

The "not invented here" syndrome is a third obstacle that kills many an idea. Every new innovation replaces someone's previous innovation. And the previous innovator(s) may see it as an affront or threat to their idea and work to prevent it.

4. Fear of Unemployment

Job insecurity often kills innovation. Blue-collar workers commonly resist any innovations to improve productivity because they fear layoffs. Who in their right mind is going to innovate themselves out of a job? And what sane middle manager or white-collar worker is going to support a downsizing effort that puts them out of work?

5. Experts

Surprisingly, experts who are thoroughly familiar with a subject or problem often raise barriers to innovation. Experts tend to know all the reasons why something can't be done. Their over-familiarity and previous successes with a problem can blind them to seeing newer, better ways to solve it. The famous inventor Charles Kettering once remarked, "When I was research head at General Motors and wanted a problem solved, I'd place a table outside the meeting room with a sign: *Leave slide rules here.*" If I didn't do that, I'd find someone reaching for his slide rule. Then he'd be on his feet saying, 'Boss, you can't do that.' "

6. Doing Everything by the Book

An overly cautious work climate that stresses doing things by the book and penalizes intelligent mistakes produces few, if any, innovations. One sure way not to make mistakes is not to try anything new. Yet progress is impossible without mistakes. As Peter Drucker put it, "The better a man is, the more mistakes he will make. I would never promote into a top-level job any man who was not making mistakes . . . otherwise he is sure to be mediocre."

7. Red Tape

Bureaucracy with all its delays, bottlenecks, and procedures kills many a good idea. All the rules and regulations of bureaucracy usually require any innovation to conform to rigid requirements and run a gauntlet of committees, policies, and procedures. Yet many of the best ideas don't fit the mold. They break it. Those few innovations that survive are often so modified and/or delayed that their effectiveness is severely diluted. The axioms that "a camel is a horse designed by a committee" and "an elephant is a mouse built to government specifications" illustrate the point.

8. Past Success

One of the most dangerous barriers to innovation is success. When we are successful, we tend to get dogmatic in our thinking and believe that we have found the best way. Henry Ford's success in mass producing one standard model car led to his famous remark, "The customer can have a car in any color as long as it's black." Yet that same policy almost cost Ford the business when General Motors started offering options and color choices to the customer. There is no best way and there will always be newer, better ways.

9. The Nature of the Beast

Finally, innovation by nature is very risky and loaded with failure. And nobody likes to fail. Less than five percent of all new ideas ever result in a new product or service, and less than ten percent of those that do are successful. Innovation involves lots of strikeouts, a few base hits, and an occasional home run that compensates for all the strikeouts a hundred fold. Very few are going to step up to the plate on their own initiative in the face of such odds.

FIVE STRATEGIES FROM SUCCESSFUL INNOVATORS

Despite all the barriers, some companies, such as 3M, Merck, General Electric, Rubbermaid, and others, are masters at the art of innovation. What's their secret? Actually there aren't any great secrets, nor is it a matter of luck. Rather, these companies see innovation as an important key to growing their business just like marketing, production, or customer service. They realize that innovation, like other crucial functions, needs to be encouraged, nurtured, and—most importantly—managed.

The following are five strategies that innovative companies use to keep them on the leading edge. The strategies are simple and practical, and virtually every one of them can be put to use to benefit any size or type of business.

1. Demand and Expect Innovation From Everyone

Like just about everything in business, innovation happens when the people at the top make it a priority and put pressure on people to deliver it. Just as most companies have sales, production, or financial goals, innovative companies have innovative goals.

Perhaps the most well known example is 3M Corporation's 25 percent rule, which requires that 25 percent of the revenue of each division come from products that have been on the market less than five years. And it's much more than just a lofty goal that's stated and forgotten. To put some teeth into the rule, meeting the 25 percent test is a key factor in determining management bonuses.

In 1985, 3M's health-care division was deriving only 12 percent of its revenue from products less than five years old. The heat was on, and the division was given 18–24 months to come up with an array of new, profitable products. Product teams were formed and came up with some winners. One is a sheet that soaks up grease from microwaved bacon. Another is a superabsorbent packing material that can be used for shipping blood samples. One team member came up with the idea after reading an article about postal workers' fears of handling blood shipments due to the AIDS epidemic. Not surprisingly, new product sales for the division rebounded to above the 25 percent level.

Rubbermaid, Inc., a Wooster, Ohio, manufacturer of housewares, toys, outdoor furniture, and office products requires that 30 percent of its revenue come from products launched in the past five years. That's no mean feat, when you consider that the company manufactures 4,700 products. In the ferocious retail world where 90 percent of new products die, Rubbermaid claims to have a success rate of 90 percent. During the 1980s, Rubbermaid's sales and earnings growth averaged 15 percent per year.

Other examples abound. Johnson & Johnson derives 25 percent

of its sales from products less than five years old. And the figures get even more impressive in rapidly changing industries like computers. More than 50 percent of Hewlett-Packard's sales come from products less than three years old.

Most companies don't think twice about demanding performance in meeting sales, production, or financial targets. Yet relatively few demand innovative performance. Then they wonder why the company lacks innovation. Innovation is hard work, and unless you ask for, measure, and demand it, you aren't going to get it.

2. Innovate From Core Competencies

Simply put, innovative businesses develop unique strengths and build on them. For example, they usually target relatively few markets that they know extremely well. Merck, America's most admired corporation according to *Fortune* magazine, gets 84 percent of its sales from pharmaceuticals. Eighty-four percent of Toyota's revenue is from automobiles, and 89% of Boeing's is from aircraft. Instead of trying to be all things to all people, innovative companies focus their efforts on developing products and services in markets they know best.

Similarly, a company that is technology-based gains the innovative edge by developing products based on a core technology that they know extremely well. At first glance, it seems like 3M sells products with nothing in common. But sandpaper, masking tape, magnetic tape, roofing materials, and Post-it notes all are created from 3M's core technology: applying a closely controlled layer of material on a flexible base.

Other examples abound: Canon's core technology is optics; Honda's is engine based; Motorola's is wireless communications; Intel's is microcomputer components and related products. By committing themselves to a core technology and working to stay on the leading edge, innovative companies are first to market with the latest products. Instead of having to compete for market share with existing products, they can often create an entirely new market with entirely new products.

3. Your Best Research Partner Is Your Customer

You can have the finest technology and the most innovative minds in the world. But unless you make or provide what the customer wants to buy, you're building bridges to nowhere. Business gets very profitable when the in-depth strengths of the business team up with the in-depth knowledge of the customer. Before you build a better mouse trap, it helps to know if anybody wants to buy one.

Most of us believe that new product ideas are generated in the research labs of private corporations and universities. Not so, according to Eric von Hippel of the Massachusetts Institute of Technology. In his research, von Hippel discovered that approximately 80 percent of all product innovations are initiated by the customer in an attempt to solve a problem.

Innovating with the customer begins with staying in close contact with the customer, along with observing and listening to him. One of 3M's war stories illustrates the point. During the 1920s, Richard Drew, a 3M inventor, noticed that painters on automobile assembly lines were having a hard time keeping borders straight as they painted two-toned cars. Drew returned to the lab and invented masking tape.

Simply talking to customers and asking them what they want may be a good starting point, but it isn't nearly enough. You have to know your customers well enough to know what their problems and wants are, and then provide new solutions. In the early eighties, you didn't hear anyone saying, "What this office needs is a fax machine." Someone in the office products business understood that there would be huge demand for a moderately priced, desk-top-size device that would transmit documents instantly via telephone. Similarly, people didn't ask for VCRs, microwave ovens, remote-control televisions, and CD players before they hit the market. It isn't enough to simply ask the customer what he wants. You have to take him on as an innovative partner, and work with him to provide the products and services he wants.

Spending time in the trenches with customers where they use your products and services can pay big dividends. One company committed to this approach is United States Surgical, a highly successful manufacturer of operating-room equipment. At least once every ten days one of their sales reps visit every one of the 5,000 hospitals in the U.S. where surgery is performed. The reps gown up, go into the operating rooms, and coach surgeons in the use of instruments that the company makes. At the same time, they listen to doctors to find out what they like, don't like, need, and don't need. Due to the close contact with surgeons, United States Surgical was quick to pick up on the rapidly rising trend in laproscopic surgery and owns about 85 percent of the booming laproscopic surgery instruments market.

The traditional approach to new product development is to spend a fortune designing, producing, and marketing a product that we hope the customer will buy. In a rapidly changing world that can be both time- and cost-prohibitive. Three popular ways to reduce the cost and time of innovating are through customer-focus groups, creative prototypes, and design-for-response.

The purpose of a focus group is to enable a business to gain a better understanding of customer likes, dislikes, and wants. The group usually consists of seven to ten typical customers, and a moderator whose purpose is to guide the discussion and get the other members of the group to relax, open up, and express themselves candidly. What do they like most about doing business with your company? What do they dislike most? If they could make one change to improve the business for them, what would they do?

Would they like your products and/or services to be better? Faster? Cheaper? Virtually every business can benefit from the feedback provided by meeting regularly with a customer-focus group.

A more aggressive, faster way to innovate with the customer is through creative prototyping. Simply put, a prototype is a crude mock-up or working model of a new product idea.

With creative prototyping the name of the game is "Get physical fast." A working model of a new product idea is quickly designed and given to a select group of customers to evaluate. The customers' feedback is used to refine and design a second prototype. The customer is given the second prototype, provides feedback, and the cycle of refinement and feedback continues. Once the prototype is refined to the point that the customer loves it, the product is produced and put on the market. It's a quick way to test new product ideas without risking a lot of money. Instead of being the end product of the innovation process, the prototype becomes the building block that drives the innovation process.

Innovative companies rely heavily on creative prototyping to spot and refine winning new product ideas. Sony used it in designing "My First Sony" (a popular line of children's electronics), by having their industrial designers interact with children as the children tried out the prototypes. And 3M let customers tell them all the possible uses and applications for their Post-it technology, resulting in a wide variety of successful Post-it products.

Design-for-response is still another effective technique for quickly determining what the customer will buy. Using this approach, several models or versions of a new product are placed on the market to see which ones sell best. For example, Seiko brings out hundreds of models of watches every year. Those that sell well stay in production. Those that don't are dropped. The production process is flexible and designed so that new products can be inexpensively produced. Similarly, Sony produces a wide range of Walkman models from a core platform to see which models are the best sellers. The winners are kept and the losers are dropped. The strength of design-for-response is that you aren't relying on customers to tell you what they want. Instead, you learn from what they actually buy.

In a rapidly changing world, thinking of the customer as someone you study and then sell to can be very dangerous. One reason Japanese companies are quicker to market with the latest products is because they don't emphasize marketing research. Instead, they concentrate on getting products to market quickly and then make changes and improvements with successive models based on what the customer tells them. What matters most isn't the product or service, but the customer's relationship to the product or service and the value they perceive. When properly carried out, making the customer a creative partner is a win/win.

4. Innovate With Small, Entrepreneural Teams

When it comes to innovation, the typical large organization shoots itself in the foot. Marketing research tells the engineers what they *think* the customer wants. Engineering then designs the product and throws it over the wall to:

- Manufacturing, who says, "You expect me to build this?"
- Finance, who says, "It costs too much."
- Marketing, who says, "The packaging is all wrong."
- Sales, who says, "It won't sell."

Once again, everyone has their own agenda and no one has the customer's agenda. With such an approach, it's no wonder that so many innovations fail in the marketplace.

One way large, innovative companies get around the size problem is through entrepreneural work teams. Such a team might consist of people from sales, a technical area, manfacturing, marketing, and finance. The team is totally responsible for taking a product idea and guiding its development from conception to completion. And team members are rewarded on the basis of the product's success.

One secret to Rubbermaid's high-success rate with new products lies in their entrepreneural teams. Each team consists of five to seven members from various backgrounds. They work together as a single team, rather than as a member of different functional departments, to design a product that the customer wants. Unhampered by bureaucracy, they concentrate their efforts on the small details and fine points of what makes a good, marketable product and get it to market faster. (Much more about work teams in Chapter 8.)

5. Create an Innovative Climate

Former IBM Chairman Thomas Watson, Jr., warned his managers of the dangers of bureaucracy by telling a parable about wild ducks. One autumn while flying south, a flock of wild ducks stopped to rest, and a duck lover fed them so well that they abandoned their journey. Seduced by all they could eat, the ducks soon forgot how to forage for food, and some became so lethargic they could no longer fly. Instead of being beautiful wild ducks, they became fat, lazy pets.

The moral of the story is that you can make wild ducks tame, but it's hard to make tame ducks wild. Watson realized that the best ideas and innovations usually come from company "wild ducks," who aren't likely to fit well into a mold of schedules, procedures, and corporate bureaucracy. In a company known for stringent dress codes, Watson's goal was that IBM have a climate where wild ducks could continue to be wild and thrive.

Innovative companies may look like all the others on the surface. But within the company they take steps to create a climate that fosters innovation. Here are some things they do that may help you make your work climate more innovative:

• *Encourage experimentation.* At 3M, anyone in the company can spend up to 15 percent of the workweek doing whatever he or she wants as long as it's product related. One of the greatest successes to come from this practice was the invention of Post-it notes, an idea that earns 3M hundreds of millions of dollars annually. Hewlett-Packard urges its researchers to spend up to 10 percent of their time on pet projects and gives them 24-hour access to labs and equipment.

You don't have to be in new product development to experiment. It's estimated that every Wal-Mart store tries up to 250 small experiments each day. It's one way department managers learn what does and doesn't work and is an outgrowth of the late Sam Walton's action-oriented, "ready-fire-aim" approach to retailing.

• *Tolerate mistakes and failure.* Remember that innovation is a numbers game. Insisting that every new idea be a home run only guarantees that nobody will step up to the plate. There's nothing wrong with mistakes and ideas that don't work as long as we learn from them and don't make them twice.

Often an unsuccessful innovation is a springboard to a successful one. In 1922, a 3M inventor tried to develop a sandpaper that could be used for shaving as an alternative to razor blades. The idea bombed, but it led to the development of waterproof sandpaper, which found a huge market in the auto industry. It's been said that Japanese companies never abandon a new technology but reserve it for a future application. The late George Bernard Shaw remarked, "When I was a young man I found that nine out

of ten things I tried didn't work. So I did ten times more work."
Take the same approach to innovation.

• *Set aside seed money for innovation.* Allocate anywhere from
5 to 15 percent of gross revenues to new ideas and experiments.
That way the business always has money to innovate without
betting the company store. Innovative companies set aside seed
money and provide grants to employees to develop promising
ideas.

• *Support your champions.* Champions are the wildest of wild
ducks. They are the ones who believe so strongly in an idea that
they will move heaven and earth to see it become a successful
reality. Virtually every successful innovation is the product of
what Peter Drucker calls "a monomaniac with a mission."

Champions can be impatient, nonconforming, intolerant, ob-
noxious, and extremely difficult to work with. And those are their
good points. But they are essential to innovation. Listen to them.
Support them. Celebrate and recognize their successes. Tolerate
and support their honest, unsuccessful ideas. And someday when
they hit one out of the park, you will be very, very glad you did.

• *Keep divisions small.* Size can kill innovation. At 3M, when a
division reaches $250–$350 million in sales, it is split up. Other
companies find that getting more than 200 people under one roof
tends to hurt innovation. Whatever rule of thumb you use, be wary
of the danger of size.

• *Relax formal rules.* Dress codes, time clocks, neat desks, and
a highly structured work environment aren't conducive to innovation. Build opportunities for humor and fun into the workplace.

Encourage people to relax and be themselves. If they want to work at home and the job permits it, let them do so. Give them deadlines and expect their best effort. But don't tell them how to do the job unless they ask. Original ideas come from original people. As H. Ross Perot noted, "Eagles don't flock; you find them one at a time."

• *Provide opportunities for interaction and solitude.* Innovative companies have learned that one of the best ways to get lots of new ideas is to get people with diverse backgrounds, training, and interests to interact with each other. People generate more ideas when they interact.

One company that has profited handsomely from this discovery is General Electric. The 1,800 researchers working at GE's research hub in Schenectady, New York, are encouraged to interact informally and trade ideas. Researchers are asked to sit with different lunch partners each day in the cafeteria and talk to people from different disciplines. On Friday evening, there is a "free beer and pretzels party." It's another occasion for people to get together, relax, and trade ideas. One innovation to come from all this informal interaction has been the creation of a new plastic that conducts electricity.

At the same time, GE researchers are encouraged to do much more than interact with other researchers. They are encouraged to think like entrepreneurs and shop their ideas throughout the company. As a result, they often find commercial applications for their ideas that are vastly different from the idea's original purpose. An invention to protect coal-spraying nozzles in an experimental locomotive ended up spawning a new generation of energy-saving light bulbs. And a medical diagnostic technology for imaging the human body found a second application as a cost-saving device for inspecting jet engines. The cross-pollinating of ideas and applications is enabling GE to create and commercialize more new products.

While interaction is crucial to an innovation, it's also important to remember that every new idea is the product of a single brain. Provide people with the opportunity and a place to isolate themselves when they need to think things through.

• *Reward your innovators.* Whether it's the launching of a whole new product line or a minor idea that saves a dollar a day, find a way to recognize and reward your innovators. What gets measured and rewarded gets done and repeated.

The 3M Company rewards its innovators by treating them like entrepreneurs. When a 3M employee has a new product idea, he or she recruits an action team of people from various backgrounds to work full-time on it. Team members from technical areas, manufacturing, marketing, and finance work full-time, deciding how to design, manufacture, and market the product. All team members are rewarded as the new product becomes increasingly successful in the market place. When sales reach the $5 million level, the originator is promoted to project manager, $20 to $30 million a department manager, and division manager at about $75 million. A separate track with commensurate rewards is available to scientists who don't want to manage.

HOW TO CREATE AND HARVEST GREAT IDEAS

Innovation and creativity aren't the same things. Creativity means coming up with great, new ideas. Innovation means turning those ideas into working realities. Creativity is imaginative, exciting, and fun. Innovation is hard work. To be an innovator takes a lot of both.

Every successful innovation starts with a great idea. And you get great ideas by generating lots of ideas and choosing the best ones. The process is much the same way a photographer gets a great photograph. The more shots he takes, the better the chances of a terrific picture. Let's look at two key ways to create more great ideas at work.

1. Teach Everyone How to Generate New Ideas

Anyone can learn to generate ideas on demand with the application of a few good idea-generating techniques. Creativity is a normally distributed human ability. Everybody has some, although some have more than others. Everyone can learn to produce more good ideas by consciously applying the following techniques:

• *Use the idea-generating cycle.* The creative process goes through a somewhat predictable cycle that occurs over varying periods of time. To generate good ideas, practice these five steps:

    I. First insight—You have a product or service you want to improve or a problem you want to solve and this step is when it first occurs to you.

   II. Preparation—Do your homework and learn as much as you can about the problem. Read, talk to others, and collect as much information as you can.

 III. Incubation—The easy part. Forget about the problem and let your subconscious work on it. Sleep on it. Forget about it. Work on something else. Give your subconscious time to work.

 IV. Illumination—That exciting, joyous moment when a great new insight or idea bubbles up from your subconscious. It may happen while driving, showering, or after awakening in the middle of the night.

V. Verification—Illumination is great stuff but very unreliable. You have to judge the new idea objectively under a bright light to see if it's worth pursuing. Get an outside opinion from someone who can be objective. Try your idea out on a customer. Few ideas will survive the test of good judgment. Good judgment comes from experience. Experience comes from bad judgment. Learn from other people's experiences whenever you can.

• *Question the status quo and challenge assumptions.* Creative people never accept the status quo as the best or correct way. Everyone believed the earth was the center of the universe and flat until Copernicus and Columbus challenged popularly held beliefs. There will always be numerous ways to improve your products, services, and the way you work. Your job is to find them before the competition does. Here's a checklist devised by a Stanford professor to jump-start your imagination. Take whatever it is you're trying to improve and ask:

- Is there a new way to do it?
- Can you borrow or adapt?
- Can you give it a new twist?
- Do you merely need more of the same?
- Less of the same?
- Is there a substitute?
- Can the parts be rearranged?
- What if we do just the opposite?
- Can ideas be combined?

• *When you see a great idea, adapt it.* Borrowing and adapting ideas is a favorite tool of creative thinkers. Einstein got many ideas for his theory of relativity while working in a Swiss patent office. Eli Whitney conceived the concept of the cotton gin by watching a cat trying to catch a chicken through a fence. George Thomas conceived the roll-on deodorant applicator by borrowing the idea from a ballpoint pen. Keep your eyes and ears open for great ideas that can be applied where you work.

• *Get a different point of view.* According to William James, "Genius, in truth, means little more than the faculty of perceiving in an unhabitual way." To get a new idea often requires looking at the same old thing in a brand-new way. The story of city engineers trying to determine how to dislodge a truck wedged beneath an underpass illustrates the point. True to their profession, they were looking at blueprints and making stress calculations when an observing child asked, "Why don't you let the air out of the tires?" New ideas come from new paradigms. Don't get trapped by habitual thinking.

• *Get yourself an idea bank.* There s a lot of truth to the old saying that nothing under the sun is totally new. But all of those old things can be combined in infinite ways, and that is the essence of how to be creative. Create an idea bank of clippings, photographs, and articles. When you observe a great idea, write it down and put it in the bank. When it's time to generate ideas, pick out a few at random and see if you can combine or rearrange any of them. As author John Steinbeck put it, "Ideas are like rabbits. You get a couple and learn how to handle them, and pretty soon you have a dozen."

• *Intuition is important.* In 1960, Ray Kroc bought a small hamburger enterprise called McDonald's for $2.7 million. His lawyer called it a "bad deal," but, according to Kroc, "I felt in my funny bone it was a sure thing."

Hunches and intuition play a large part in the creative process, because very often a hunch is a collection of facts stored at
the subconscious level. Whenever you have a strong, gut-level
feeling about an idea, ask yourself, "Is it possible that I've
managed to gather information about this without consciously
realizing it?" If the answer is yes, pay close attention to it. But
a word of caution: Confusing hunches with wishful thinking
is courting disaster. Don't confuse what you feel with what
you want.

• *Be alert for the unexpected*. It's called serendipity, the knack
of making unexpected discoveries, and creative people and companies know how to capitalize on it. For example, in the 1950s, a
group of 3M researchers were trying to develop a synthetic rubber
for jet aircraft hoses. A beaker containing the trial substance broke
and some of it spilled on a lab technician's tennis shoe. No
standard cleaning solvent could remove it. The substance never
became synthetic rubber, but with further refinement it became
Scotchgard fabric protector, a very successful 3M product. As
Marshall McLuhan wrote, "All discoveries in art and science
result from an accumulation of errors." The best ideas and opportunities turn up at the most unexpected times and places. Keep
your eyes and ears open for them.

• *Think up now, judge later*. To think up and judge ideas simul-
taneously is like stepping on the accelerator and brake of your car
at the same time. When you're generating ideas, go for quantity.
As Linus Pauling remarked, "To have a good idea you have to
have a lot of ideas."

Those are idea-generating techniques. Here's a great idea-
harvesting technique for the workplace.

2. Start a One-Idea Club

Being an innovator means a whole lot more than coming up with breakthrough products and services. While major innovation is important, it's equally important to find new ways each day to make small improvements in the way everyone does their job. The cumulative effect of small innovations and improvements can have immense impact and needs to be encouraged.

One very effective way to encourage people to be creative is to form a one-idea club at work. Everyone on the payroll is a member and is asked to think up or find at least one idea for improving the business or their work. If they go to a seminar or training program, their job is to come back with at least one new idea for improving their work. If they visit a successful business, their assignment is to come back with one idea that can be applied to improve their job or the business. If a problem needs to be solved, ask everyone to suggest at least one idea and give them plenty of praise and positive reinforcement when they do.

It's absolutely amazing how creative people can be when given the opportunity and incentives. Here are four actual and very amusing examples from what I call my One-Idea Club Hall of Fame:

- Have you ever been asked to write a reference letter for someone you didn't feel comfortable recommending? The next time that happens, use the pro-forma letter that Robert Thornton, professor of economics at Lehigh University has created for such a situation. It goes like this:

Dear Madam or Sir:
I am pleased to say that this candidate is a former colleague of mine. In my opinion, you will be fortunate to get this person to work for you. I recommend him with no qualifications whatsoever.

No person would be better for the job. I urge you to waste no time in making this candidate an offer of employment. All in all, and without reservation, I cannot say enough good things about him, nor can I recommend him too highly.

• A hair-stylist, who charged $31 for a haircut, had a Fantastic Sam's Family Haircutters (a discount haircutting chain) open a shop across the street. A huge sign at Fantastic Sam's read, "We give six-dollar hair cuts." The stylist countered with a sign that read: "We fix six-dollar haircuts."
—From Jeff Slutsky, Columbus, Ohio

• At a posh California resort near the Del Mar Racetrack, the management was plagued by prostitutes, who placed business cards on doors, drink machines, and other locations throughout the resort. Management assigned people to pick up the cards as soon as they spotted them. But the ladies of the evening just kept on distributing the cards promoting "Surfer Girls."

After spending a lot of time and energy, a complete and immediate solution was found for under $10. A rubber stamp was made and a hotel staffer was instructed to stamp the back of each business card and leave it right where they found it. The stamp read, "First Hour Free."
—From Gary Beals, San Diego, California, and Ed Rigsbee, Westlake Village, California.

• A small instruments manufacturing company manager (names withheld to protect the guilty) saved a sale, a customer, and perhaps the business with this one idea. A very major customer placed a very large order for specialized instruments with an iron-clad deadline date. If the deadline wasn't met, the customer would cancel the order and all future business. To lose the order meant a possible bankruptcy situation.

The problem was that an essential component for the instruments ordered would not arrive until the day after the deadline. What was the manager to do?

He solved the problem by filling boxes with plastic peanuts and shipping them to the customer. This gave the company time to receive the missing part and they worked night and day to build the instruments.

The customer received the empty boxes on the deadline date. When the manager received the expected telephone call from a very angry customer, his reaction was, "What? . . . No! . . . I can't believe it!!! . . . Somebody's really gonna hang for this . . . Yes, of course, we'll get you a replacement shipment off immediately . . . and I mean *today!*"

—from Ron Wright, Union Lake, Michigan

While that manager isn't likely to be inducted into a Business Ethics Hall of Fame, he did save the business and the customer. Yes, necessity *is* the mother of invention. If you don't have a one-idea club, get one. A rapidly changing world requires a commitment to continuous improvement through innovation.

4 Do It With Quality

The things that take the most time are the things that go wrong.

—DON POVEJSIL

Want to speed up output, reduce costs, motivate your colleagues, and get your customers to love you? Here's an excellent rule of thumb: *Do it right the first time.* That, by definition, is doing it with quality—our fourth commandment for winning more business in less time.

If focusing on the customer is the foundation of a business, then committing to quality represents the infrastructure upon which the business is built. Here's what happens when you do it right the first time:

• *Output goes up.* The fastest way to do a job is to do it right the first time. Time and effort previously devoted to repairing and correcting errors is used to produce more goods and services. Managers spend more time on productive tasks rather than checking for errors. Think about this: If you can't find the time to do it right the first time, where will you find the time to do it again?

• *Costs go down.* Doing jobs right the first time lowers production costs by channeling previously wasted energy, materials, and overhead into producing goods and services for the customer. Warranty costs go down. Labor costs go down because it takes fewer workers and managers to produce the same amount of output. According to quality expert Joseph Juran, "By and large, on the order of 20 to 30 percent of a company's activities are wasted doing things that should have been done right the first time." It is estimated that the typical factory spends 20 to 25 percent of its operating budget in finding and fixing mistakes.

• *Morale goes up.* Jobs become easier because no one has to do the same job over or correct someone else's mistakes. Work becomes more pleasant and less stressful as people feel successful, confident, and proud from knowing how to solve problems and do the job right. And when morale goes up, employee turnover goes down.

• *Customers multiply and come back.* This is the big payoff. When everyone does the job right, customers get what they want, the way they want it, when they want it. Satisfied customers create more customers, more profits, a more competitive business, and more job security.

In recent years quality has taken on the mantle of a business religion. Everybody worships at the altar of quality, and everyone wants to achieve superior quality for one simple reason: Without it your business is in trouble. In a world where customers have so many choices, there is enormous pressure to give them the greatest possible value while keeping costs as low as possible. As Fred Smith, Founder and CEO of Federal Express, remarked, "Anybody who's unwilling to spend on quality is really mapping a blueprint for liquidation."

In the period after World War II and until 1973, America's economic success came largely from economies of scale. The key to success was quantity, or "He who makes the most toys wins." There was virtually no foreign competition, and little pressure to produce high quality, and many businesses developed some very sloppy habits.

As the world entered the information age and foreign competition emerged, mass production lost much of its effectiveness. Many corporations tried to prop up their numbers with "smoke and mirrors"—financial techniques such as takeovers, leveraged buy-outs, junk bonds, and the like. The battle cry of the eighties was "He who dies with the most toys wins." But in a world where the customer rules, "He who makes the best toys wins." And that's what quality is all about.

CLEARING UP THE QUALITY CONFUSION

With so many experts, consultants, books, and seminars on the topic, it's not surprising that there is a lot of confusion and misunderstanding about what quality is. When we talk about high quality, are we all talking about the same thing? One way to clear up a lot of the confusion is to distinguish between process quality, perceived quality, and total quality management:

• *Process quality* is doing jobs right the first time. It means consistency, reliability, and conformity to requirements. Whether it's building products on an assembly line, shipping finished goods, purchasing raw materials, or resolving customer complaints, everything done in organizations involves a process. No matter what the job is, the more we do it right the first time, the higher the level of process quality. The key is to decide what "it" is and conform to those requirements. For example, at Domino's, delivering a hot pizza in thirty minutes or less is "it" for the delivery person.

• *Relative-perceived quality* is customer satisfaction, or how customers rate the overall quality of a business relative to its competitors. It is the single greatest key to long-term profitability. Customers come to a business with preconceived expectations about what they're going to get for their money. The key to high-perceived quality is to exceed those expectations and give the customers the most value per dollar as they perceive it.

Both types of quality are essential and interrelated. To achieve high-perceived quality, we have to know what customers' wants and expectations are and decide how to satisfy and exceed them. Why sell efficiently made, high-quality products that nobody wants to buy? It's like winning the battle and losing the war.

Assuming we know what they want, the next step is to produce products and/or services that consistently delight customers. To accomplish this at the lowest possible cost requires doing jobs right the first time. More mistakes means wasted materials, delays, shoddy products, frustrated workers, and unhappy customers.

When we combine process and perceived quality with a mandate to improve continuously, we have:

Total quality management—An ongoing strategy for providing increasingly higher levels of customer satisfaction through continuous improvement.

Continuous quality improvement is important because customers expect increasingly higher levels of quality and will continue to do so. Quality is a moving target where what's good enough today won't be good enough tomorrow. Achieving and sustaining superior quality is a tough, never-ending job. But in today's world, it's the only job worth having.

As you may have gathered, quality and speed are actually two sides of the same coin. Practicing all of the other nine commandments of speed improves quality. And improving quality increases speed. Achieving high quality and high speed is the ideal combination, because it means people do what should be done, how it should be done, and when it should be done to satisfy and delight the customer.

Many businesses spend a lot of money to implement quality-improvement programs only to find themselves frustrated by the results. The problem is that quality is not a program. It's a whole new way of doing business that involves difficult change. Too many businesses treat quality like a Band-Aid cure, while the truth is to make it work usually takes major surgery. If that's the case where you work, consider the following keys to doing it with quality as a guide to help you get better results.

QUALITY STARTS AT THE TOP

When it comes to quality, the person at the top can't blow an uncertain trumpet. Everything said and done from the top down must continually reinforce the message that quality is crucial for survival and prosperity in today's world. While quality experts may disagree on the finer points of quality, they all agree that nothing improves unless there is a wholehearted, consistent, unwavering commitment to quality from senior management.

Corning, Inc. Chairman James R. Houghton delivers essentially the same quality sermon about 50 times a year every year to various Corning offices and plants: Quality is paramount. Focus on the customer. Worker participation. Be world-class. Quality. Quality. Quality.

And the Corning commitment to quality goes far beyond words.

Following his address, Houghton meets with managers for a serious performance review session on quality. To reinforce the quality message, everyone from top management to factory workers is held accountable and rewarded for achieving quality objectives. While delivering the same message may get tiresome to Houghton, the results are remarkable. He began the process in 1983, and from 1986–1991 Corning's operating profits jumped 111 percent.

When quality efforts fizzle out, and most of them do, it's usually because management talks about the importance of quality, but doesn't demand and reward it. As pollster Daniel Yankelovich put it, "When it comes to quality, management gives their people mixed messages. On one hand, they give a lot of lip service to it. But if you look at the reward systems, if you look at incentives, if you look at what people are paid to do and rewarded to do, it's not for quality."

Employees are very quick to pick up on how deeply the people at the top are committed to quality. If top-management bonuses and employee incentives and rewards are tied to quality goals and improvements, the business is on the right track. Otherwise you can expect quality to become just another passing fad. What the leadership says is important. What it does is critical. Linking quality improvements to pay gets everyone's attention.

QUALITY IMPROVEMENT IS ACHIEVED THROUGH PEOPLE

In the early 1980s, General Motors spent over $60 billion on automation designed to eliminate assembly-line workers. The assumption was that if quality was poor, workers were to blame. Get rid of the workers and you improve quality. It didn't work, and GM wasted a lot of money. The workers weren't the problem. The management system was.

Quality improvement becomes possible when workers are treated as part of the solution rather than as part of the problem. As I mentioned earlier and will no doubt mention again, the person doing the job usually has the best ideas for improving the job.

That was one of the insights that enabled Cadillac to be the first automobile manufacturer to win the Malcolm Baldrige National Quality Award in 1990. Instead of blaming the workers, Cadillac changed the management system. Instead of treating workers and the union as the enemy, Cadillac realized that the competition was the enemy and the customer was the prize. Instead of managers managing and workers working, management gave workers more control over how they performed their jobs and asked them for their ideas for improving quality. In the spirit of everyone working together as a team to please the customer, jobs, processes, and products were redesigned with terrific results. It sounds simple on paper, but to accomplish such a transformation involved nothing less than a massive cultural change.

To be sure, technology can and usually does play a significant role in quality improvement. Indeed, a worker is no better than his tools. Many routine office and manufacturing jobs are done better and faster by computers, robots, and the like. But technology is not a substitute for good management. And good management begins with leaders creating a climate where caring, thinking, motivated people work together in the spirit of teamwork, harmony, and improvement.

MANAGE YOUR CUSTOMERS' EXPECTATIONS

The final measure of quality lies in the hearts and minds of customers. It's not what you know, but what your customers perceive that counts. Customer perception is everything, and, as I mentioned earlier, the key to high-perceived quality is to find out what they want and exceed their expectations.

While you can't control your customers' perceptions, you can take specific steps to manage their expectations. The general rule for managing expectations is *underpromise and overdeliver*. Too many companies do just the opposite. They spend a fortune in advertising, telling the customer how wonderful their quality is when it really isn't. All they are doing is spending money to raise the customer's expectations. And raising expectations only increases the odds of a disappointed customer. Why spend money to shoot yourself in the foot? Don't tell the customer how great you are. Show him!

If it takes three days to do a job, promise it in five. If you have to give an estimate, add ten percent to it and pleasantly surprise the customer when they get the bill. Additionally, here are four other strategies for building a quality image in your customers' eyes.

1. Little Extras Make the Big Difference

Do something extra to remind the customer that you're taking very special care of him. Businesses with great reputations don't just provide high quality. They also know how to tactfully remind the customer that he or she is their top priority.

When I bought my Seville STS from Sewell Cadillac, I mentioned that I was leaving for Australia the following month on a two-week speaking trip. They immediately volunteered to baby-sit my car for me while I was out of town. I dropped the car off at the dealership the evening before I left. They kept the car inside, serviced it, washed it, and delivered it to my home the evening before I returned—all at no additional charge. Sewell Cadillac understands that the sale really begins when the customer says "yes."

People believe that Wal-Mart has succeeded through rock-bottom pricing, but that's only part of the story. At every Wal-Mart a "greeter" welcomes everyone entering the store and assists parents in putting infants in the shopping carts. When customers ask where a particular item is, they aren't merely told. They are taken to the item by a Wal-Mart associate. When customers sign a check or credit-card slip at the checkout, they are thanked by name. As Sam Walton put it, "The nicest-sounding word to any person is his own name, especially in this day when computers are making numbers out of us." All those little things positively shape the customer's perception of quality, especially when the prices are so low.

John Gremer of San Jose, California, has two great examples of how to do something special for the customer and increase sales at the same time. The first involves a contracting business that installed residential products, such as roofs, gutters, ceiling fans, roof vents, and insulation. California law requires that all such products installed carry a one-year warranty on labor. Eleven months after installation, every customer was called and asked, "We value your business, and your warranty expires next month. Is there any work you need done while it's still under warranty? Or is there any other way we may be of service?" The calls generated a small amount of warranty work and a huge volume of new work and referrals.

The second example comes from the plumbing, electrical, heating, and air-conditioning repair business. Customers requesting repair work are charged a minimum amount for a service call, which is usually an hour's labor. A frequent customer complaint is, "The repairman charged me $50 for an hour's labor and was only here 40 minutes." The problem was solved by telling the technicians to complete their work, and explain what was done and why. Then the technician would say, "Mrs. Smith, there's still 20 minutes left on your service call. Is there anything you'd like me to check in your plumbing, electrical, or heating system while I'm here?" According to Gremer, the complaints stopped, technicians felt like heroes, and sales increased anywhere from 15 to 30 percent.

2. Minimize Perceived Waiting Time

Nobody likes to waste time waiting for service. In fact, one study reports that when more than four people are waiting in a checkout line, the odds are high that a fifth person will just leave.

A number of businesses have learned how to take the agony out of waiting. One recent study of doctors' offices found that if the doctor, or another primary care provider, walked into the examination room, made immediate eye contact with the patient, smiled, shook hands, and gently touched the patient in a friendly manner, the patient's estimate of waiting time decreased 50 percent.

At Walt Disney World, lines are curved to make them appear smaller. Customers are diverted with entertainment while they wait in line, and signs such as "10 minutes from this sign" tell customers how long they have to wait. The actual waiting time from the "10 minute" sign is about seven minutes. Time really flies when ten minutes goes by in seven.

3. Train Your Customers With a Service Guarantee

When Domino's promises delivery in "30 minutes or free," or Federal Express promises your parcel delivered "absolutely, positively overnight," they are teaching customers what to expect. At the same time they are telling employees what level of performance is necessary to do it right the first time. Instead of making a vague promise to deliver quality, they offer an objective benchmark for measuring performance. The customer knows what to expect, and the employees know what the customer expects. The key to high quality lies in meeting and exceeding those expectations.

Sooner or later, every business that wants to succeed must guarantee the quality of its work. It's better to make a specific promise up front. In addition to teaching customers what to expect and employees what to do, a quality guarantee increases sales. As the late Sam Walton wrote, "The two most important words I ever wrote were on that first Wal-Mart sign: SATISFACTION GUARANTEED. They're still up there and they have made all the difference."

4. Do a Quality Overkill When Things Go Wrong

Like it or not, your customers aren't thinking about you when you deliver great products complemented with great service. They just take it for granted. But when something goes wrong, that's when they are thinking about your business—a lot. Smart companies realize this and use customer disappointments, mishaps, and complaints as opportunities to strengthen customer loyalty by showing him just how much they value him. Here are two examples of what I mean:

> A New Orleans businessman had a very important evening interview in Houston. He flew to Houston that morning and ripped the trousers of the only suit he had brought. In desperation, he called Fred Aubert, a salesman at the suburban New Orleans clothiers where he bought the suit. Fred immediately got the customer's measurements from the file, took an identical pair of pants from another suit, altered them accordingly, and put them on the next flight to Houston. The customer received the trousers in time for the interview, and Fred won another customer for life. He is the top salesperson in the world for Hart-Marx Clothing and has held that distinction for 19 consecutive years. As his manager remarked, "Fred never loses a customer. They either die or move away."

Dr. Neil Baum, a New Orleans physician, doesn't charge his patients for an office visit if they have to wait more than 20 minutes past the appointment time to see him. You can just imagine how quickly this turns an inconvenienced patient into a walking advertisement. He gets a tremendous number of patient referrals. Don't you wish your doctor did that?

When handled correctly, it's possible to create more customer loyalty from a problem than if the problem had never occurred. Let the customer know how sorry you are they have been inconvenienced. Then do something special for them to compensate them for the problem. And finally, where appropriate, follow up with a telephone call to make sure that all is well. Happy customers come and go, but angry ones accumulate and can literally destroy a business. A good quality overkill plan transforms a potential liability into a loyal customer and a walking referral service. In addition to continuing to buy from you, a satisfied complainer, on average, will tell five people good things about your company.

QUALITY IS PREVENTION, NOT INSPECTION

There was a time when we believed that higher quality increased costs. The problem was that quality wasn't being achieved by preventing errors but rather by inspecting products and throwing out those not up to standard. When you do that the waste is tremendous and the cost of doing business escalates. As W. Edwards Deming pointed out years ago, "You don't inspect quality into a product."

A quality program that focuses on preventing mistakes, rather than inspection, lowers costs for a simple, common sense reason: *Problems create problems.* Quality trainers are fond of quoting the "1-10-100" rule attributed to George Labovitz and Y. S Chang. The rule states:

For every dollar your company spends to prevent a quality problem, it will spend ten to inspect and correct the mistake after it occurs. And if the customer discovers the quality failure, it will probably cost about one hundred times more to fix the problem than it would have cost to prevent the problem from occurring in the first place.

When Federal Express insists on doing jobs right the first time, they realize that a single glitch can snowball into a multitude of problems. If a truck driver is late, the package sorting is delayed and that, in turn, means the planes won't leave on time. All of which jeopardizes the Federal Express service guarantee of delivering all priority-one packages to the customer by 10:30 A.M. the following morning.

When American executives toured Japanese manufacturing plants in the late seventies and early eighties, they were surprised to find that any worker working on a huge assembly line could stop the entire line to fix a problem whenever he spotted one. Back in the States, the traditional American assembly line moved at a predetermined pace. Errors were to be detected and/or corrected by quality-control inspectors at the end of the line. Today we understand how wasteful and costly that practice is. Quality is like health care. The best and cheapest medicine is preventive medicine. Do it right the first time.

Global electronics giant Motorola knows firsthand the value of doing it right the first time. In 1974, its suburban Chicago plant was manufacturing television sets and averaging 150 defects per set. Motorola sold the plant to Matsushita of Japan in 1974, and by 1979 the plant was averaging only four defects per set.

When several officers complained of the company's product quality, Motorola made a major commitment to change its entire organization to a quality culture and has had stunningly successful results. In 1988 Motorola won the Malcolm Baldrige National Quality Award and has been called "the company that can out-Japanese the Japanese," because it regularly beats its Japanese competitors in both price and quality. From 1987 to 1992, Motorola's component-defects rate dropped from 6,000 per million to 30 per million, while productivity and earnings nearly doubled. (Most American companies average between 6,200 and 67,000 defects per million.) In 1992, the defects reduction saved the company an estimated $900 million.

USE QUALITY TEAMS, TERMS, AND TOOLS

Quality improvement started in manufacturing. But the greatest future gains in quality will occur in white-collar, information, and service jobs where most of us work. This means that everyone in every job from the top down must be thoroughly familiar with the definitions of quality, and know how to use the tools of quality to improve his or her job. Japan's rise from junk merchant to world-class quality leader began with American quality-control experts teaching Japanese leaders, not those on the factory floor.

The quality-improvement process is usually carried out through quality-improvement teams, who systematically look for problems to solve and better ways to get things done. The team typically uses a problem-solving format that goes like this:

1. Choose a specific problem. Why is it important? How will solving it help the customer and/or lower costs?
2. Gather specific data and information about the problem.
3. Analyze the data for possible causes.
4. Decide on a solution or solutions.
5. Plan how to carry out the solution.
6. Do it! Put the plan into action.
7. Check it. Did it solve the problem?

8. Follow up. Make sure it stays fixed.
9. Choose another specific problem and repeat the cycle.

Of course, before turning a team loose to seek out and solve quality problems, the team needs to learn basic statistical and problem-solving techniques. Quality improvement relies on gathering, measuring, and analyzing hard data and using this information as a basis for setting improvement goals. If it's worth improving, it's worth measuring.

An important term to understand is the *cost of quality*, which is simply the cost in dollars of not doing jobs right the first time. Wasted energy, labor, materials, overhead, and the lost revenue from customers who don't come back all contribute to the cost of quality. Phil Crosby said it best: "Quality is free. What costs money are the unquality things—all the actions that involve not doing jobs right the first time."

FIND AND ADAPT THE SMARTEST IDEAS

Another important term is *competitive benchmarking*, and it's one of the most popular practices in total quality management. Xerox Corporation defines benchmarking as "the continuous process of measuring products, services, and practices against the toughest competitors or those companies recognized as industry leaders." The implication is simple: *Continuously search for the best ideas and adapt what you learn to improve your products, services, and processes.*

There are several approaches to benchmarking, and they all can be helpful. One way is to look for the best practices within your own company and spread them throughout the business. For example, when Avon decided to streamline its distribution service it looked for the best practices in each of its five distribution centers and molded the best ideas into a single system of practices for all to emulate.

Another way to benchmark is to research your industry for the best ideas and adapt those. In the early eighties, Ford compiled a list of 400 features that customers said were most important in a car, and they found a car that was the best at each feature. The goal was to design a new car that matched or beat the competition in each feature. The result was the highly successful Ford Taurus and Mercury Sable of the mid-eighties.

Finally, some companies receive the best ideas and practices from totally different industries. When Xerox wanted to improve its speed and accuracy in fulfilling orders, it went to L. L. Bean, one of the best at warehousing and mail-order distribution. One of the keys to Motorola's dramatic quality turnaround came from having its manufacturing experts tour some of the world's finest manufacturing facilities. Taiichi Ono, creator of the Toyota just-in-time manufacturing system, got his best ideas from touring American supermarkets in the fifties, where he observed goods being rapidly replenished in response to sales. Everything starts with an idea. And the best products, services, and practices come from the best ideas.

BE SPECIFIC AND GO FOR THE SMALL WINS

A study conducted in 1992 by Ernst & Young for the American Quality Foundation suggests that the total quality movement in most U.S. firms is floundering. According to the study, one of the key reasons for the lack of success is that most quality programs are too amorphous to generate better products and services. It's one thing to spend a fortune on books, seminars, training tapes, and consultants to teach quality, and another thing to integrate it into the company culture. For quality to work, it has to become philosophy, habit, and the way business is carried out each day. Otherwise it's a waste of time and money.

Before people can assimilate quality principles into their work, they have to be able to relate the philosophy, principles, and techniques to their job. One way to achieve this is to give them specific quality goals. For example, during the eighties, health-care giant Johnson & Johnson based its quality program on "doing things right the first time." While that's a good general definition and starting point for understanding quality, Johnson & Johnson found it wasn't specific enough. So they established three specific quality goals: boosting customer satisfaction, reducing product introduction time, and cutting costs. Each of the 166 operating units were then told to "apply the principles of total quality management in a way that makes sense for them." Instead of teaching everyone the same quality concepts across the board, classes are tailored to teach people the specific skills and tools they need to improve quality in their particular departments and jobs.

One way to increase the effectiveness of quality training is to form quality teams of people who normally work together and teach them the tools and techniques of quality in a learning-by-doing format. As soon as the team learns the tools, assign them a quality goal. Have them apply what they learn right away to solve a quality problem where they work. This reinforces the usefulness of the training and lessens the odds of learning in a vacuum.

While the ultimate goal is to achieve major improvements in quality, it's also important to think small and go for the small wins. The biggest improvements in quality usually aren't the result of doing any one thing a thousand percent better. Rather, it's the accumulation of doing thousands of things one percent better. That's why it's important to think small and go for the small wins. Japan knows the value of thinking small. According to the National Association of Suggestion Systems, in 1987 the typical U.S. financial return for an idea was $5,000, but in Japan the average idea was worth $130. However the U.S. averaged only .13 ideas per person while Japan averaged 24. Little improvements add up to big dollars, and Japan's reputation for quality speaks for itself.

INVOLVE EVERYONE AND BE PATIENT

When I say involve everyone I mean it: suppliers, customers, managers, workers, and anyone who can help you deliver the greatest value to the customer at the lowest possible cost. Let your customers tell you what they want. Then tell your suppliers what you need, how you need it, and when you need it to take care of your customers. And finally, remember the best ideas for improving a job come from those who do it every day.

Quality isn't something you have installed next Tuesday. It takes time, patience, attitude, and commitment. A study by the U.S. General Accounting Office of high-scoring applicants for the Malcolm Baldrige National Quality Award revealed that total quality management can take up to three years before having an impact. And any meaningful impact can take up to six years in a work climate that's high in bureaucracy and low in trust.

What's really important is to realize that total quality isn't a program or a project, but rather a whole new philosophy and way of doing business for most businesses. It's a strategy, not a result, a journey, not a destination. There is no way to quality. Quality is the way.

5 Get Rapid, Accurate Feedback

The most successful man in life is the man who has the best information.

—BENJAMIN DISRAELI

A dog food company's sales were poor. The sales manager decided to solve the problem with a motivational rally. He assembled the sales force, ran up to the front of the room, and screamed out:

"What dog food is the most nutritious?"
"Ours is!" shouted the reps.
"Who has the finest advertising campaign?"
"We do!" was the reply.
"And who's the best sales force in the industry?"
"We are!" answered the group.
"Well," said the sales manager, "if our dog food is the most nutritious, and we have the best advertising campaign, and if you are the best sales force in the industry, then *Why Aren't We Selling More Dog Food?*"
After a long pause, a single voice in back of the room replied:
" 'Cause them dogs don't like it!"

Like so many of us today, the sales manager wasn't adequately informed. As long as "them dogs don't like it," motivating the

94

sales force is going to be an exercise in futility. The sales force doesn't need motivating. Management needs a dose of reality. And that's what good feedback provides.

It's the paradox of our time. In the middle of the information age, too many of us are information poor. At a time when we are inundated with reports, data, statistics, facts and figures, so many of us lack the simple and sometimes obvious insights that can make our businesses, careers, and lives so much more successful.

Stop for a moment and think about successful persons or businesses that you are familiar with. While there may be any number of reasons why they are successful, all have one trait in common. Successful people and businesses are good at solving problems and capitalizing on opportunities. They know how to spot a problem or opportunity, create and evaluate their options, and take action. Most important of all, they are reality driven. They insist on seeing the world as it is, rather than how they would like it to be. They realize that truth, like surgery, sometimes hurts in the short run but cures in the long run.

Turbulent times require that we maintain a constant vigil to knowing what our customers, suppliers, competitors, bosses, and associates are thinking and doing. Information such as this enables us to win a lot more business in less time. The right information allows us to build relationships, spot opportunities, capitalize on our strengths, correct weaknesses, and nip a potential crisis in the bud. But being poorly informed in today's world is akin to a soldier walking unknowingly through a minefield. Which leads to the most important rule of rapid, accurate feedback:

DON'T SHOOT THE MESSENGER
MAKE SURE THAT BAD NEWS TRAVELS QUICKLY
TO THOSE WHO CAN DO SOMETHING ABOUT IT

When Harold Geneen sat at the pinnacle of ITT, he gave his senior executives a two-word directive: No surprises. Like most smart bosses, Geneen realized that good news almost always travels fast and usually isn't as crucial. Far more important is how quickly problems and potential problems are detected. It's much easier to put out a small, smoldering fire before it escalates into a raging blaze. A problem rarely erupts into a crisis without some warning. Harold Geneen made it clear to his lieutenants that keeping their jobs depended on keeping him informed of any potential problems that could throw the company into a crisis. If there was any bad news, it was their job to know about it and tell him—fast.

All of us need a good early-warning system for bad news and potential problems so we can do something about them. Unfortunately, the higher you rise in an organization, the more difficult it becomes to rely on the formal communication system to know what's happening. Almost no one likes being the bearer of bad news, and even fewer want to deliver it to the boss. You aren't going to find out the real story by reading memos, because the people who write those memos lie. They don't mean to lie. But the fact is no one is likely to put anything in writing that makes them look bad in the boss's eyes. As one of the older directors told a new company president, "Congratulations. You have heard the truth for the last time."

According to the late An Wang, founder of Wang Industries, "Ask employees what's wrong, not what's right." If you are a boss, don't just accept bad news. Encourage and demand it as long as it's factual and timely. Encourage customers, employees, suppliers, and anyone with information that affects the business to bring forth bad news quickly. As one Bank of America executive put it, "We only kill the messenger if he's late with the news."

THE BEST WAY TO FIND OUT WHAT'S HAPPENING

If you really want to know what's going on in the world of your customers, associates, suppliers, competitors, or whoever, the best way is simple and obvious. *Find out what's happening in person.* There's no substitute for experiencing reality firsthand. Get out where the rubber meets the road and talk to customers and front-line employees. Better yet, if you are a manager, spend some time working on the front line, listening to customers and associates and asking for suggestions on how you can help them do their jobs better. Mystery-shop your own business and the competition. How does your business measure up? Call up your own company and your competitors with a complaint, question, or order and see how you get treated. Meet face-to-face with anyone you want to forge a better working relationship with to find out what's happening and how you can be more valuable. First-hand information is first-class information.

Until shortly before his death, Sam Walton spent many days traveling the country in his private plane and dropping in on several Wal-Mart stores each day. Today every senior manager at Wal-Mart spends at least two days a week visiting the stores. During the early years of General Motors, GM Chairman Alfred Sloan would leave Detroit every three months and spend a week working as a salesman or assistant service manager at several dealerships around the country. Working in the field enabled Sloan to spot market trends and customer preferences before GM's customer research did. Bill Marriott, Jr.'s, habit of traveling extensively to make on-site visits to Marriott properties is legendary. Time is the most precious commodity to people with such enormous responsibilities. Yet, all three found it a worthwhile investment to spend large amounts of time gathering information firsthand. There's a lesson there for all of us.

QUALITIES OF USEFUL INFORMATION

How can you tell if information is useful? In general, good business information meets the criteria listed below. If you can answer yes to most or all the following six questions about a piece of information, it's probably useful:

1. Will It Improve Relationships?

As much as some accountants, number crunchers, and information systems experts may dislike it, business is people and relationships. The customer's relationship with the business ultimately determines the success or failure of the business. How employees interact as they work together largely determines how efficient and effective a business will be. As columnist Michael Schrage writes, "The unpleasant reality is that most organizational technologists are more interested in getting the right computers to talk to each other than the right people to do so. . . . Instead of asking, 'What is the information that matters and how do we most effectively manage it?' companies must start asking, 'What are the relationships that matter and how can the technology most effectively support them?' "

2. Will It Cause Anyone to Take Positive Action?

Will the information help you, your suppliers, associates, or the company to improve performance? Will it help solve a problem or snuff out a potential crisis? Will it result in happier customers? Will it lower costs and improve sales or quality? Good information is goal-oriented and points the way to improvement.

3. Is It Factual?

The story goes that every day a man would set his watch by the clock in a jewelry store window. One day the jeweler stopped the man and said, "I see you set your watch by my clock. What kind of work do you do that demands such correct time every day?"

"I'm the watchman at the plant down the street," the man replied. "Every day I blow the five o'clock whistle."

"But . . . you can't do that," said the surprised jeweler. "I set my clock by your whistle!"

The moral of the story is that it's hard to make accurate decisions with inaccurate information. Make sure your sources are sound, objective, and reality-based rather than the product of someone's wishful thinking. As David Kindred remarked, "Never assume anything but a four and one-half percent mortgage."

4. Is It Timely?

Today's world places a premium on immediate information. The best performance feedback tells employees how they are doing their jobs as they do them. The more immediate the customer feedback, the faster we can resolve complaints and take positive action. Information technology makes it possible to stay on top of inventory levels, shifts in customer buying patterns, cash flows, and a myriad of other details as they happen. In a world where speed is profit, timely information makes faster, better decisions possible.

Buick has discovered a simple way to get immediate improvements in product quality. Teams of Buick engineers gather complaints from customers and dealers and relay them directly to the manufacturing plants. For example, complaints of leaks in the rear window of new LeSabres were immediately traced to a robot that left gaps in the window sealant. The problem was corrected the same day.

5. Will It Go to Those Who Can Make the Best Use of It?

Remember, good information enhances relationships and enables the recipient to take positive action. Procter & Gamble's Duncan Hines angel food cake factory provides a good example. Factory workers are given letters from customers who have a problem with the mix and encouraged to contact them directly. One factory worker telephoned a customer whose angel food cake didn't rise to try and find out why. Did she beat the mix long enough? At what temperature was the cake baked? Putting those who make the product in touch with the final customer is a practice that benefits everyone.

6. Can It Be Summarized and Expressed Concisely?

While it's important to have all the details if needed, the best information can also be summarized and portrayed to communicate the big picture. For example, customer satisfaction is frequently measured by asking lots of customers a series of rating-scale questions. But to make sense of the information requires getting an average score on each question, category of question, or an overall index of customer satisfaction. Whenever information can be expressed concisely, numerically, or graphically, it makes it easier to grasp and use as a basis for future action. It's much like the scoreboard at a ball game. While the coaches may be collecting a lot of detailed statistics for future analysis, the scoreboard provides the overall picture and a basis for immediate action.

In summary, good business information does three things. It serves as a reality check, strengthens and supports essential relationships, and provides a basis for making decisions and taking positive action.

THE FOUR MOST IMPORTANT THINGS YOU NEED TO KNOW ABOUT YOUR CUSTOMERS

A successful business owner who is a great believer in customer feedback once told me of an interesting experience that he had as a customer.

It seems that he was a passenger on Eastern Airlines. The flight was late, the plane was dirty, and the service was horrible. He commented on the poor service to the lady sitting next to him.

"What do you do for a living?" she asked.

"I own my own business," he replied. "What do you do for a living?"

"I'm the customer-service representative for Eastern Airlines. I read all the complaint letters that people write," was her answer.

"Oh, really?" said the man. "I've always wanted to know something. What do you do with those letters?"

She replied, "We read them and throw them away."

It may be an oversimplification, but I believe the above anecdote goes a long way toward explaining why this man had a very successful small business while a once-successful, international airline goes broke. It may also help explain why an airline like Southwest has enjoyed successful growth and profits during hard times in the airline industry. Every week Southwest Airlines invests over 1,500 man-hours writing personal responses to the over 1,000 letters it receives from customers each week. Southwest CEO Herb Kelleher believes customer letters are the best system he has found for monitoring airline performance. In 1992, Southwest had the highest ratings in customer satisfaction, baggage handling, and on-time performance of any major U.S. airline.

Here are four crucial things that every business needs to know about its customers.

1. Who They Are

Do you know what customers you're trying to serve? What's their age range? Education level? Income level? What problems do they look to your business to solve for them? The more you can pin down who your customers and potential customers are, the better the chances of creating products and services of high value to them.

American Express makes it their business to know 450 things about each cardholder. Through a process of surveying customers and test marketing new ideas, they can determine which cardholder services make a difference to customers and which don't. For example, customers place a high value on toll-free, 24-hour phone services, which cost relatively little for American Express to provide. Amexco also breaks down the universe of cardholders into segments based on income and lifestyle characteristics and then sells customized services to appeal to each group. Limousine pickups are offered for upscale platinum card members. Extra travel insurance is offered to senior citizens who place a premium on security. And a special magazine is offered to students.

In today's world, smart selling means targeting a specific segment of customers (who may be as small as one) and forming an ongoing partnership with each one. This requires finding out as much as you can about them and then offering the products and services they want. Knowing who they are is the first step.

2. What They're Thinking

Success in business isn't determined by what we make, how hard we work, or who the president of the company happens to be. *Success in business is determined by what the customers and potential customers of the business think and feel about the business. Period.* Businesses that make the effort to listen to their customers and give them the most value per dollar (as the customer perceives it) are the winners. Those that don't can only hope the competition is equally inept at customer empathy. Here are several popular ways to find out what your customers are thinking:

• *Do a mini-survey.* Finding out what your customers think doesn't have to be a complex process. When my car is serviced at Sewell Cadillac, I get a call the following day from the service advisor asking if the problem has been solved. A few days later I get a telephone survey call from the dealership that asks me three simple questions that take less than thirty seconds to answer: 1) Was my car ready when promised? 2) Are the charges more, less, or the same as the estimate quoted? and 3) Is this the second time I've brought the car in for the same repair? Periodically the service advisor calls just to ask how I like my car and to find out if I'm having any problems. All of this takes very little time, and Sewell Cadillac gets invaluable feedback on what their customers are thinking. When there is a problem, they know about it and can take action to solve it And when everything's okay, asking those questions builds perceived value by subtly reminding the customer that he is getting great service. What are the three most important questions you would like to ask your customers?

• *The comment card* (Figure 1) is another useful vehicle for gathering customer feedback. It usually consists of about ten to

FIGURE 1. *Alaska Airlines' Customer Comment Form*

WELCOME ABOARD ALASKA AIRLINES!

All of us at Alaska Airlines care about you and want your flights with us to be convenient and enjoyable in every respect. Our objective is to keep Alaska Airlines the best airline in the West. Your suggestions and comments on the service you've received from us will help us achieve that objective. So please take a few brief moments to complete this questionnaire and let me know personally how you think we lived up to your expectations today.

Sincerely yours,

Bill McKnight

Bill McKnight
Vice President, Marketing

Flight No. _____ From _____ To _____ Date _____ Seat No. _____ First Class ☐ Main Cabin ☐

Please note your reaction to those elements of our service which you experienced on this trip.

	Excellent	Good	Satis-factory	Unsatis-factory	Poor
MAKING YOUR TRAVEL ARRANGEMENTS					
Courtesy and helpfulness of reservation agents........	☐	☐	☐	☐	☐
PRIOR TO YOUR FLIGHT					
Handling of airport check-in....................	☐	☐	☐	☐	☐
Courtesy and helpfulness of check-in agents...........	☐	☐	☐	☐	☐
Professional agent appearance....................	☐	☐	☐	☐	☐
Handling of seat assignment....................	☐	☐	☐	☐	☐
Baggage check-in service....................	☐	☐	☐	☐	☐
DURING YOUR FLIGHT					
Cabin appearance and cleanliness....................	☐	☐	☐	☐	☐
Attendants pleasant and attentive....................	☐	☐	☐	☐	☐
Professional attendant appearance....................	☐	☐	☐	☐	☐
Clarity of cockpit announcements....................	☐	☐	☐	☐	☐
Cabin staff announcements:					
Clarity....................	☐	☐	☐	☐	☐
Alaska Airlines connecting flight information.........	☐	☐	☐	☐	☐
Meal quality....................	☐	☐	☐	☐	☐
Meal quantity....................	☐	☐	☐	☐	☐
Food temperature....................	☐	☐	☐	☐	☐
Timely and gracious meal presentation....................	☐	☐	☐	☐	☐
Beverage service....................	☐	☐	☐	☐	☐
UPON YOUR ARRIVAL					
Baggage:					
Care in handling....................	☐	☐	☐	☐	☐
Timeliness of delivery....................	☐	☐	☐	☐	☐
Convenience in making connecting flights.............	☐	☐	☐	☐	☐
Helpfulness and clarity of Alaska's airport signage...	☐	☐	☐	☐	☐

SPECIFIC REMARKS: _____

_____

_____

_____

Name (Mr./Mrs./Ms.) _____ Representing _____ Title _____
Please circle one   First   Last

Address (Company/Residence) _____
Please circle one   Street   City   State   Zip

Are you a Mileage Plan member? ☐yes ☐no Member Number _____ Daytime Telephone _____

WHAT IS THE PURPOSE OF YOUR TRIP TODAY?

☐ Business	☐ Pleasure	☐ Other _____

Thank you for flying with us today and for commenting on our service. Please drop in any mailbox. Postage is prepaid.
© Alaska Airlines, Inc.   Reprinted with permission of Alaska Airlines

twenty short "how do we rate?" questions and provides a quick overview of strengths and weaknesses as seen through the customers' eyes. The weakness of comment cards is that they tend to be answered by those who had a very good or very poor experience. You're sure to hear from the ten percent who love you and the ten percent who hate you. But the 80 percent who are making or breaking your business aren't as likely to answer. Personally handing the card to the customer is a good practice that elicits a higher response. Most comment cards are passively left on restaurant tables, checkout counters, or in hotel rooms.

• *A comprehensive survey* takes more of the customer's time but can provide an enormous amount of valuable information. Alaska Airlines' confidential survey (Figure 2) is one of my favorite examples, because it provides the airline with a huge amount of information about the customer and the competition in a relatively short amount of time. Passengers who complete and mail in their confidential survey within five days after their flight have their names entered in a contest. Five names are drawn and each winner receives two round-trip tickets.

• *Customer focus groups* (discussed in Chapter 3) are an excellent feedback tool that Sewell Cadillac has put to good use. While fewer customers participate, taking the time to find more about what customers think and want has enabled Sewell to add services that matter to the customer. Every customer has a personal service advisor who fosters a doctor-patient type of relationship and keeps "medical records" on their car. The service garage is open all day on Saturdays, and loaner cars for customers is a standard practice. Adding such services has dramatically increased Sewell's market share.

• *Mystery shoppers*, people posed as customers who evaluate the business, can provide useful insights. Dr. Neil Baum employs

FIGURE 2. *Alaska Airlines' Confidential Survey*

WIN A FREE ROUND TRIP FOR TWO
ON ALASKA AIRLINES

In a continuing effort to improve the quality of **Alaska Airlines'** service, we feel it is important to listen to what our passengers have to say. Please assist us in this endeavor by completing this confidential survey.

David L. Palmer
Assistant Vice President Marketing

We are entering all participants in a contest to win a free round trip for two on Alaska Airlines. Five winners will be selected. Trips will be awarded from the nearest Alaska Airlines gateway city to any other city served by Alaska Airlines, except Russia. All you have to do is return this form within five days of your flight. See rules on last page for details.

1. Please write in your flight number _____

2. Please write in today's date _____

3. In which city did you board this flight today? _____

4. In which city will you leave Alaska Airlines today? _____

5. Which phrase or phrases best describe your reasons for taking this trip? **(Circle as many as apply)**

   1 Business
   2 Visiting friends or relatives
   3 Vacation
   4 Government/military business

   5 Accompanying family member on business
   6 Personal emergency
   7 Other _____

6. How many nights in total will you/did you spend away from home on this trip? **(Circle choice)**

   1 None
   2 1 night
   3 2-4 nights
   4 5-7 nights

   5 8-13 nights
   6 14-20 nights
   7 21+ nights

7. Who are you traveling with today? **(Circle as many as apply)**

   1 No one
   2 Spouse
   3 Children 12 or under
   4 Children over 12
   5 Other relatives

   6 Friends
   7 Business associates
   8 Organized group
   9 Other _____

8. Who selected Alaska Airlines for today's flight? **(Circle as many as apply)**

   1 I did personally
   2 Travel agent
   3 Secretary
   4 Company travel department

   5 Family member
   6 Business associate
   7 Government/military
   8 Friend or relative
   9 Other _____

9. If you are on vacation, is this flight part of a packaged tour (e.g., sightseeing tour, cruise, etc.)? **(Circle choice)**

   1 Yes   2 No

FIGURE 2. *Alaska Airlines' Confidential Survey (continued)*

10. If you had anything to do with selecting Alaska Airlines for this flight, how important would you rate each of the following factors in making your decision to fly with Alaska Airlines on today's flight, using a scale where 1 = Not At All Important, 2 = Not Very Important, 3 = Somewhat Important, 4 = Important, and 5 = Very Important?

		Rating			
01 Airline reservations agent	1	2	3	4	5
02 Attitude of employees	1	2	3	4	5
03 Convenient schedules	1	2	3	4	5
04 Flight attendant service	1	2	3	4	5
05 Frequent flyer program	1	2	3	4	5
06 Inflight food and beverage	1	2	3	4	5
07 Leg room	1	2	3	4	5
08 Lower airfares	1	2	3	4	5
09 On-time performance	1	2	3	4	5
10 Overall airline performance	1	2	3	4	5
11 Quick baggage delivery	1	2	3	4	5
12 Seating comfort	1	2	3	4	5
13 Ticket/gate personnel	1	2	3	4	5

11. Where have you overnighted (or have you stayed) on this trip? **(Circle as many as apply)**

01 Not staying overnight	06 Cruise
02 Hotel	07 Camping
03 Motel	08 Resort
04 Condominium	09 Work site
05 With friends/relatives	10 Other _____

12a. Have you, or do you plan to rent a car on this trip? **(Circle choice)**

1 Yes (Go to 12b)   2 No (Go to 13)

12b. If so, which rental car company or companies did you/will you rent from? **(Circle as many as apply)**

1 Alamo	5 Hertz
2 Avis	6 National
3 Budget	7 Thrifty
4 Dollar	8 Other _____

13. Including today's trip, how many **total air round trips** have you made during the last twelve months (including all airlines)? **(Please circle choice under "Q13" below)**

14. Including today's trip, how many total air round trips have you made <u>on all airlines on this route</u>? **(Please circle choice under "Q14" below)**

15. Including today's trip, how many total **air round trips** have you made during the last twelve months <u>on Alaska Airlines on this route</u>? **(Please circle choice under "Q15" below)**

Q13		Q14		Q15	
1	1	1	1	1	1
2	2-4	2	2-4	2	2-4
3	5-9	3	5-9	3	5-9
4	10-14	4	10-14	4	10-14
5	15-19	5	15-19	5	15-19
6	20+	6	20+	6	20+

FIGURE 2. *Alaska Airlines' Confidential Survey (continued)*

16. **NOT** including today's flight, please tell us if you have ever flown on the following airlines; if so, write in the number of **air round trips** you've taken on each one in the last 12 months, and indicate if you belong to their frequent flyer program. **(Circle as many as apply)**

	Have Flown	(Fill In Number) Round Trips In Last 12 Months	Member Frequent Flyer Program
Alaska Airlines	1	_____	1
America West	2	_____	2
American Airlines	3	_____	3
Continental Airlines	4	_____	4
Delta	5	_____	5
Northwest Airlines	6	_____	6
Southwest	7	_____	7
TWA	8	_____	8
United	9	_____	9
US Air	10	_____	10
MARKAIR	11	_____	11

17. Please rate your <u>overall</u> impression of Alaska Airlines **(not just this flight)** and **TWO** other carriers from the list with which you are most familiar. For each characteristic below, use a scale where 1 = Poor and 5 = Excellent. **(Please write in "Other Carriers" number where provided)**

OTHER CARRIERS

* AMERICA WEST	= 1		* SOUTHWEST	= 6
* AMERICAN	= 2		* TWA	= 7
* CONTINENTAL	= 3		* UNITED	= 8
* DELTA	= 4		* US AIR	= 9
* NORTHWEST	= 5		* MARKAIR	= 10

	Rating
1) Flight Attendant Service	
* Carrier Number: _____	1 2 3 4 5
* Carrier Number: _____	1 2 3 4 5
* Alaska Airlines	1 2 3 4 5
2) On-Time Performance	
* Carrier Number: _____	1 2 3 4 5
* Carrier Number: _____	1 2 3 4 5
* Alaska Airlines	1 2 3 4 5
3) Inflight Food and Beverage	
* Carrier Number: _____	1 2 3 4 5
* Carrier Number: _____	1 2 3 4 5
* Alaska Airlines	1 2 3 4 5
4) Airline Reservations Agent	
* Carrier Number: _____	1 2 3 4 5
* Carrier Number: _____	1 2 3 4 5
* Alaska Airlines	1 2 3 4 5
5) Seating Comfort	
* Carrier Number: _____	1 2 3 4 5
* Carrier Number: _____	1 2 3 4 5
* Alaska Airlines	1 2 3 4 5
6) Lower Airfares	
* Carrier Number: _____	1 2 3 4 5
* Carrier Number: _____	1 2 3 4 5
* Alaska Airlines	1 2 3 4 5
7) Convenient Schedules	
* Carrier Number: _____	1 2 3 4 5
* Carrier Number: _____	1 2 3 4 5
* Alaska Airlines	1 2 3 4 5
8) Leg Room	
* Carrier Number: _____	1 2 3 4 5
* Carrier Number: _____	1 2 3 4 5
* Alaska Airlines	1 2 3 4 5
9) Attitude of Employees	
* Carrier Number: _____	1 2 3 4 5
* Carrier Number: _____	1 2 3 4 5
* Alaska Airlines	1 2 3 4 5
10) Overall Airline Performance	
* Carrier Number: _____	1 2 3 4 5
* Carrier Number: _____	1 2 3 4 5
* Alaska Airlines	1 2 3 4 5

FIGURE 2. *Alaska Airlines' Confidential Survey (continued)*

		Rating				
11)	Ticket/Gate Personnel					
	• Carrier Number: _____	1	2	3	4	5
	• Carrier Number: _____	1	2	3	4	5
	• Alaska Airlines	1	2	3	4	5
12)	Frequent Flyer Program					
	• Carrier Number: _____	1	2	3	4	5
	• Carrier Number: _____	1	2	3	4	5
	• Alaska Airlines	1	2	3	4	5
13)	Quick Baggage Delivery					
	• Carrier Number: _____	1	2	3	4	5
	• Carrier Number: _____	1	2	3	4	5
	• Alaska Airlines	1	2	3	4	5

18. Thinking about today's flight, how would you rate Alaska Airlines in the following areas? **(Please use a scale where 1 = Poor and 5 = Excellent)**

		Rating				
01	Ticket/gate personnel	1	2	3	4	5
02	Convenient schedules	1	2	3	4	5
03	Airline reservations agent	1	2	3	4	5
04	Flight attendant service	1	2	3	4	5
05	Lower airfares	1	2	3	4	5
06	Quick baggage delivery	1	2	3	4	5
07	Attitude of employees	1	2	3	4	5
08	Leg room	1	2	3	4	5
09	Overall airline performance	1	2	3	4	5
10	Frequent flyer program	1	2	3	4	5
11	Seating comfort	1	2	3	4	5
12	Inflight food and beverage	1	2	3	4	5
13	On-time performance	1	2	3	4	5

19. From the list below, please indicate the number of each type of vacation you take by air in a typical year.

		# Taken
1	Weekend trips/a few days	_____
2	One week	_____
3	Two weeks	_____
4	Three weeks	_____
5	More than three weeks	_____

20a. What, if anything, do you like most about Alaska Airlines?

_____

_____

20b. What, if anything, do you like least about Alaska Airlines?

_____

21. How close to the scheduled departure time did your plane leave the gate? **(Circle choice)**

1	Within 5 minutes	4	30-44 minutes
2	6-14 minutes	5	45-59 minutes
3	15-29 minutes	6	1 hour or more

The following information will be used for analysis and classification purposes only, and will not be identified with you personally at all. (Please circle appropriate response)

22. Into which of the following categories does your age fall?

1	Under 18	4	35 to 44	6	55 to 64
2	18 to 24	5	45 to 54	7	65 or over
3	25 to 34				

23. Are you . . .

1	Male	2	Female

24. What is your current marital status?

1	Single	3	Divorced/separated
2	Married	4	Widowed

FIGURE 2. *Alaska Airlines' Confidential Survey (continued)*

25. Please indicate the highest level of education you have received.

1 Did not graduate from high school
2 Graduated from high school
3 Some college
4 College graduate
5 Postgraduate college study/degree

26. Which of the following best describes your current occupation? **(Circle one)**

01 Company management	08 Craftsman, mechanic
02 Professional	09 Fisherman
03 Executive	10 Homemaker
04 Teacher/professor	11 Airline employee/
05 Sales representative/	eligible family/
agent	travel agent
06 Government/military	12 Student
07 Secretary, clerical,	13 Retired
office worker,	14 Currently not working
sales clerk	15 Other _____

27. Which of the following categories best describes your total annual family income?

1 Under $24,999	4 $50,000 - $99,999
2 $25,000 - $39,999	5 $100,000 or more
3 $40,000 - $49,999	

Winners will be notified within two weeks of the drawing. Please print the following information carefully.

Name _____

Address _____

City _____ State _____ Zip _____

Phone (___) _____

mystery patients to visit and evaluate his medical practice in urology. The waiting room, examination rooms, and all personnel, including Dr. Baum, are scrutinized in detail and evaluated by mystery patients. The mystery patients also spend time in the waiting room, listening to real patients and any comments about the doctor and the practice. They also present common problem scenarios to the staff, such as forgetting their checkbook, and evaluate how diplomatically they get treated. When the mystery patient visits, no one, including Dr. Baum, knows who they are.

Only when Dr. Baum tells the patient he wants to perform a physical examination does the mystery patient identify himself. Using this and a number of innovative, patient-focused techniques, Dr. Baum's practice grosses double the income of an average solo practice in urology.

* *The customer hot line,* a 24-hour, toll-free number, is another popular way to get more customer feedback and more sales. Customers who may not feel comfortable complaining in person, or who have a problem that needs resolving, can gain immediate access to the business and trained personnel to help solve the problem. The advent of low-cost, toll-free telephone lines puts this customer feedback tool within the reach of almost any size business.

If you use a hot line, comment card, or voluntary customer satisfaction survey, consider supplementing them with a proactive technique like focus groups, telephone calls, or face-to-face inquiries. While you're sitting back waiting for the customer to tell you what he thinks, he may just quietly take his business down the street. A typical business hears from only 4 percent of it's dissatisfied customers. The other 96 percent slip away and 91 percent of those who leave never come back.

3. What They're Buying

What customers tell you they want is important. What they buy is critical. And those aren't always the same things. For example, a restaurant's customers may say they want more low-cal and heart-healthy items. But when it comes time to order, many of these same customers opt for greasy cheeseburgers, French fries, and a shake. Customers may lie, but the numbers don't. You need to know what's selling, in what quantities, at what price, who's buying it, when they're buying it, and where it's being bought. And you need to know it ASAP.

Fortunately, information technology makes it possible for even the largest companies to capture such valuable feedback in precise detail and with incredible speed. A heavy investment in the likes of bar-code scanners, satellite equipment, and computer technology during the eighties was a major factor in Wal-Mart's phenomenal growth and success. Through a satellite that links all stores, distribution centers, and the home office, Wal-Mart feeds detailed sales information to a central computer. A 65-week rolling history is kept on line of every item stocked in a Wal-Mart or Sam's Club. A Wal-Mart executive who wants to know how a particular model telephone has sold in the past 15 months can find out in as much or as little detail as he wants. He can find out how many units sold on a specific day, in a particular store, district, region, or nationally.

Such instantaneous sales feedback provides a tremendous competitive advantage to companies that have it. Inventory and distribution costs are lowered, because only those items selling are restocked. Stock-outs and the accompanying missed sales are reduced. And customer loyalty is strengthened, because customers know that Wal-Mart will have what they want, when they want it, and at the lowest price.

4. Why They Quit

While it can be a painful exercise, one of the best ways to keep customers is to get feedback from the ones you lose. Call them. Write them. Go see them. Let them know that keeping customers delighted is your top priority.

Then, ask them why they aren't buying anymore. Do they dislike the product? Did they move away? Are they getting a better price elsewhere? Were they treated rudely or indifferently? What can be done to make things right for them? This is important feedback that every business needs to know.

Getting feedback from ex-customers has two major payoffs. First, you'll find out why they left. This gives you an opportunity to correct the problem and win the customer back. While you can't win them all, some will come back once they realize that you care. And second, feedback from ex-customers will point out flaws and weaknesses that you can correct before even more customers defect.

To be sure, you can't keep all of your customers nor should you try. Some just aren't worth it in dollars and cents. But in today's world, small increases in customer retention result in large increases in the bottom line. And this makes feedback from ex-customers a great source of profit potential. The wise learn from misfortune. Fools merely repeat it.

In summary, every business needs to know who its customers are, what they're thinking, what they're buying, and why they quit. And this feedback needs to be updated frequently, if not continuously. Otherwise, you risk having your competitors cross the finish line before you realize there's a race.

KNOW YOUR COMPETITION

Ideally, you take wonderful care of your customers. You give them what they want, how they want it, whenever they want it, at the price they want it. When you know your customers better than the competition and meet their needs better than the competition, you, in effect, have no competition. Sounds great, right? But this isn't an ideal world. And it's forever changing as the number of competitors mushroom in almost every business.

The reality of the marketplace is that someone wants your customers and is trying to take them away from you right now. If you don't stay on your toes, they will. This makes it important that you know the competition almost as well as you know your customers. More specifically:

1. Who Are Those Guys?

In earlier, simpler times, the competition was easy to spot. They sold what you sold and were probably just down the street. Technology, however, is not only shrinking the world and intensifying global competition, it's also creating competition between previously noncompeting businesses and creating brand-new competitors. For example, the fax machine puts telephone companies in direct competition with the Post Office and Federal Express. The VCR has created a whole new industry—video rentals—to compete for the entertainment dollar. Cable television has created numerous competitors for the major networks.

It's getting harder and harder to identify the competition, but failing to do so is courting disaster. Many of the problems facing Sears today were caused by its failure to recognize Wal-Mart and K-Mart as competitors.

The best way to identify the competition is through your own customers and ex-customers. Ask your loyal customers who they would buy from if you weren't around. Ask them where they shop if they can't get what they want from your business. Ask them who they think your competition is. Talk to customers who quit and find out where they went. Similarly, if the volume of a customer's business drops, find out if they're buying a substitute product or service elsewhere. Don't just assume you know who the competition is. Find out.

2. What Are Your Competitors' Strengths and Weaknesses?

Assuming your competition is correctly identified, the next step is to know their competitive strengths and weaknesses relative

every system requires only two components: a goal and a way to keep score. You need to know what you want to achieve and a performance indicator to tell you how you're doing.

You may be already using one of the most basic (and most useful) performance feedback tools: the daily "to do" list. When you write down the five or six things you want to accomplish in a day and rank them in order of importance, you're setting goals. As you complete each item and scratch it off the list, you're getting feedback. At the end of the day you have a scorecard to tell you how you did. If every item has a line through it, you did great! If you didn't get much done, you know that too, and it serves as a warning indicator. Adjustments are needed to get you back on track to doing what's most important.

Cypress Semiconductor Corporation of San Jose, California, requires each of its over 1,400 employees to set goals each week. While that may not sound very innovative, what is unique is that all employees commit to achieving their goals by a certain date, enter them into a computerized data base, and report whether they have achieved their previous goals. This computerized version of Management by Objectives provides a guide to the future and an objective record of the past. In addition, management can find out very quickly who's achieving their goals and who isn't. Those doing well can be singled out for recognition and rewards, and those who aren't can be counseled to determine what needs to be done to get them on track. Every week 6,000 goals become due, and, according to President and CEO T. J. Rodgers, "Our ability to meet those goals ultimately determines our success or failure."

The process of setting specific goals and performance indicators should begin by getting some verbal feedback from those you work with. Some questions you may want to ask your boss are:

- What do you feel are the one or two most important results that I need to focus on achieving in my job?

- What do you see as my greatest strengths and weaknesses?
- If you were I, what would you work hardest on improving?
- What can I do that I'm not doing now that would benefit you, our customers, and the company?

Motion picture executive Louis B. Mayer remarked, "I don't want yes-men around me. Tell me what you think even if it costs you your job." If you're in a management position, you need candid feedback too. It can be hard to get face-to-face feedback, and you may want to use an employee survey form that allows anonymous answers. Some questions you may want to ask subordinates and your peers are:

- What can I do to help you do a better job?
- What can I do to make us both more valuable to our customers?
- What do I do that gets in the way of your being more productive?
- What's the greatest obstacle you face in trying to do your job?
- If you were in my shoes and could make only one change to make your job more effective, what would you do? ("I'd resign" is not an acceptable answer.)

Finally, if you deal with suppliers, don't forget to get input from them too. In this case, you're the customer and it's the supplier's job to keep you happy. Nevertheless they're an essential part of your team, and you need to work closely with them in a world where speed is profit. Some questions for suppliers might be:

- What kind of information can I provide you with that would make our company easier to work with?
- What do I need to know about your operation so we can better coordinate our activities?

- Are we doing anything that makes it difficult for you to serve us?
- How can we work together to make our relationship more mutually profitable?
- What can we do to help you get orders to us faster?

To sum up the fifth commandment, get the most up-to-date, accurate feedback you can about what your customers, competitors, suppliers, and associates are thinking and doing. And there's one other source of feedback that's very important—the clock. In a world where speed is profit, knowing and improving response time is crucial. More about that in our sixth commandment.

6 Ability Means Agility

Market share is an anachronism. What drives success today is market responsiveness.
—JOHN THORBECK, President and CEO,
George E. Keith Company

- It used to take Motorola three weeks to build and ship an electronic pager after receiving an order. Today they can do it in two hours.
- It once took Hewlett-Packard 53 months to develop a new printer and bring it to market. It now takes 22 months and will soon take less than a year.
- The typical retail store replenishes its stock in the stores once every two weeks. Wal-Mart replenishes its stock an average of twice a week. This means Wal-Mart stocks the goods its customers want with one-fourth the average investment in inventory. Wal-Mart is growing three times faster than the retail industry average and enjoying twice the average rate of return on capital.
- It's common to take a month or more to get approval on a home mortgage. In 1989, Citicorp announced that approvals would be granted in 15 minutes.
- Too busy to shop for your new personal computer or the latest software? Just call Mac Connection before 3 A.M. Eastern

time and place your order. You'll receive it by 4 P.M. that same day.

- When it comes to customer responsiveness, National, a Japanese bicycle manufacturer, takes the prize. Customers can choose from a combination of 11 million different styles and sizes of bicycles and receive their made-to-order bike in two weeks. Word has it that National can actually make and deliver a customized bike in three days. But most customers wouldn't believe it so they don't promise it.

Now, think about this—what you just read is history. Those are examples of customer responsiveness from the late eighties and early nineties, not some pie-in-the-sky prediction for the future. As you read this, some of those examples are already becoming obsolete.

Agility is the new competitive edge. It means not only responding and adapting quickly, but being able to offer customers variety as well. When the customer wants you to turn on a dime, your job is to do it and give him a nickel back. You can practice all the other nine commandments brilliantly, but if you fall down on this one, all is lost. In today's world, a business without agility is in bad shape.

Slow response time is a problem with many large businesses because they grew and prospered in the more stable "bigger is better" era, when success was achieved through economies of scale, from large investments in mass production, mass marketing, and vertically integrated structures. But in today's world, bigger isn't necessarily better. In too many cases, it's just slower. The new economic realities make quality, innovation, and speed more important than cost, growth, and control.

Yet size isn't inherently a problem and has tremendous advantages. Big companies have access to more capital and other resources that enable them to achieve levels of success unavailable to smaller businesses. It's analogous to athletic competition. While speed and quickness may be essential qualities, a big, quick player beats a smaller quick player most of the time.

WHAT DOESN'T WORK

To succeed today, the corporate Goliaths need more than big company muscle. They need entrepreneurial agility, which usually means doing things very differently from the past. Unfortunately, many attempts to improve responsiveness typically begin with a number of outdated ideas, such as:

1. If Everyone Would Just Work Faster . . .

Expecting everyone to work faster or put in longer hours almost always guarantees disaster. Simply stepping on the gas isn't going to have a positive effect unless people are working like zombies. The more likely result is lower morale, higher turnover, greater absenteeism, and a subsequent decrease in quality and responsiveness.

2. Let's Automate It

Using technology to do the same old jobs the same old way is another loser. Computerizing a bureaucracy just creates more red tape that strangles responsiveness even more. Using robots to automate jobs usually doesn't work either. General Motors' multi-billion-dollar fiasco that replaced workers with robots is a classic example.

Using the powers of technology to speed up an outdated business system is like a military leader using computerized catapults and robotic archers to strengthen our national defense. The beauty of technology is that it gives us the possibility to do brand-new things in brand-new ways. And that's where quantum leaps in agility occur.

3. Let's Get Rid of the Fat

In concept, it's a great idea, and is covered in Chapter 7. Unfortunately, attempts to get rid of the fat too often translate into making across-the-board cuts that can cripple or destroy a business. What would happen to your health if you lost weight by having portions of your bones, internal organs, muscles, and fat removed in across-the-board percentages? All too often a business that downsizes ends up trying to do the same old things the same old way, with the fewer people on hand feeling overworked, underappreciated, afraid of losing their job, and burned out.

The point is simply this: Working faster, automating, and downsizing in themselves aren't going to increase agility. It's much like the problem of a cattle rancher trying to get his cattle to market faster. He can make the cowboys ride faster and put in longer hours on the trail. He can pave the trail. He can lay off some of his cowboys. But he's still taking the cattle to market via an outdated cow path when railroads, airlines, and expressways are available.

WHAT WORKS

Agile businesses do a number of things differently from their more traditional counterparts. Traditional companies stress cost control. Agile companies stress time control. Instead of mass producing goods in large batches, agile manufacturers have flexible systems with production runs as small as one. Instead of relying on mass marketing, the new breed relies more on niche marketing, micromarketing, and keeping the customer by providing outstanding service. Instead of trying to do everything, agile companies stay flexible by doing only what they do best and forming partnerships with others to do the rest. Agile companies have much leaner staffs and fewer managers. And information technology is the strategic tool that enables them to be agile, responsive, and close to the customer. Let's look now at some of the key strategies for becoming and staying flexible and quick to adapt.

1. Time Is of the Essence

"How long does it take?" That's the question every business needs to answer about every important activity and task. The traditional approach to business success is to deliver value to the customer at the lowest possible cost. The new paradigm for success today is to provide the customer the greatest value at the lowest cost in the shortest possible time. The key is to be flexible and responsive enough to give customers what they want, how they want it, when they want it. Costs are still important, but focusing only on costs can be penny wise and pound foolish.

For example, let's look at product cycle time, i.e., the total amount of time it takes to conceive, create, and get a new product to market. According to Arthur Andersen & Co., a company whose product cycle times are one-third of its competitors' will enjoy triple the profits and triple the growth.

Time is the new strategic measure, because shrinking performance times raises revenues and lowers costs. As Ralph Waldo Emerson wrote, "In skating over thin ice, our safety is in our speed." In a world where speed is profit, you need baseline measures of how long it takes to perform crucial activities, such as:

- Responding to an inquiry by a customer or prospect.
- Getting an order delivered to the customer.
- Acknowledging the customer's presence.
- Fulfilling a customer's special request.

- Resolving a customer's complaint to their satisfaction.
- Receiving inventory from suppliers once an order is placed.
- Conceiving, developing, and bringing new products and services to market.
- Changing the production process to produce a different product (changeover time).
- Billing the customer and collecting payment.
- Making management decisions.

Of course, what activities need to be measured will vary from business to business. For example, a supermarket may find it very useful to know how long customers wait at the checkout lines and how often the shelves are replenished. It would also be wise to know how it measures up against its major competitors in these time-based categories. Armed with such information, it can start looking for ways to improve inventory turnover or shrink customer-waiting times in a cost-justifiable way.

2. Improve the Whole Process Instead of the Functions

Specialization of labor was the backbone of the industrial revolution and of the tremendous economic growth we have enjoyed in the past two centuries. In 1776, Adam Smith described how one pin maker working alone could make 20 pins per day, but 10 specialized workers made 48,000 per day. Small businesses mushroomed into giant ones when they organized into specialized functions (such as finance, production, and marketing) and assigned every person, work group, and department a narrow, specialized task to perform.

The problem with functional specialization is that everybody is concerned about their piece of the puzzle, but almost nobody cares about how well the pieces fit together. Everyone is held accountable for performing their own narrow tasks efficiently and effectively while the process of making the entire process effective goes largely ignored.

In contrast, agile companies focus on improving the entire process. Rather than improving *what* gets done, they look at *how* things get done, and they often reorganize the entire process to make it more flexible. Instead of organizing around functions, agile companies frequently organize around products or customers and then redesign the entire process to be more responsive.

Let's use a hypothetical bicycle manufacturing plant as an example. A traditional factory might organize into functional departments such as stamping, welding, painting, assembling, and testing. Every bicycle made goes through each department in sequence. Particular models and colors of bikes are produced in large batches to increase efficiency and reduce changeover times and costs. Nonmanufactured parts are purchased in large quantities, warehoused in a nearby central inventory, and retrieved as needed. It's a nice, efficient procedure for predictable, stable times.

But what happens when an important retail dealer wants 500 Model A bikes in an array of colors by Tuesday and the line is set up to produce Model B blue ones? Or what happens to productivity when one department develops a bottleneck? In such an organization it's typical for parts to move from one department to another and wait days or weeks or longer until they can be used. The result is a huge hidden inventory cost and tremendous delays. And speaking of inventory, what about all that capital and space that's tied up in the huge central inventory of parts waiting to be used? It's no way to do business in a rapidly changing world.

In contrast, an agile factory sets up several small, parallel assembly lines. It locates the various activities on each line close together to insure that the bikes being made move smoothly from one sequence to the next without wasting time in the process. It schedules deliveries from parts suppliers to arrive as needed in order to keep inventory costs low. Instead of a large, central inventory, parts are kept in small bins close to the appropriate assembly line to save time. It focuses on reducing changeover and setup times for each line so it can respond quickly to changes in customer demand. Instead of relying on forecasts and hoping to sell what it makes, the agile factory keeps tabs on sales and lets the customer tell them what to make. And finally, everyone makes an ongoing effort to make small, continuous improvements and refinements in the process to make it more customer responsive. Instead of concern for a narrow task, everyone's major concern is improving the system to get quality goods to the customer ASAP.

3. Streamline the Structure

Not long ago I visited the world headquarters of a large corporation. I was immediately underwhelmed with the stifling bureaucracy, complete with paper shuffling, endless meetings, political infighting, and an endless supply of clerical and support personnel who promptly left at quitting time. It was pretty apparent that advancement here was more dependent on political gamesmanship than taking care of the customer or improving the bottom line.

It's quite a contrast to a small business in the same industry that I visited. There the atmosphere was one of unbridled enthusiasm. People talked endlessly about their latest project and how much they enjoyed their work. They considered the owner a friend as well as the boss. Everyone understood that pleasing the customer was job one and worked hard to do so. Some came to work early, left late, and frequently worked weekends—not because they had to, but because they wanted to. They were optimistic about the future and were grateful they had found such a great place to work. The contrast was striking.

Fortunately, it's possible to infuse a large company with entrepreneurial enthusiasm and agility. The strategy is simple: *Take the large business and divide it into a number of small ones, with each one focused on serving a particular group of customers or markets.* That's what Siemens, a large German electronics corporation, did in 1989. To keep the company agile, the $45 billion corporation was divided into 16 small corporations with revenues ranging from $500 million to $8 billion each year. Each corporation has its own CEO and board of directors. Every CEO has final authority in his minicorporation but must get approval on expenditures of over $10 million. As Albert Hoser, CEO of U.S. operations, put it, "We split up the big battleship into a flotilla of effectively run small ships under one admiralty."

Other large companies keep their entrepreneurial agility by subdividing whenever a division gets too large. As I mentioned in Chapter 3, when a division at 3M reaches $250 to $350 million in sales, it is split up. And Bill Gates divided Microsoft from five divisions to fifteen, with each having no more than 200 people under one roof. Whatever rule of thumb is used, the future is clear. The large company of the future is going to operate like a number of small, customer-focused businesses under one umbrella. Entrepreneurial agility is in and middle management bureaucracy is out.

4. Manage Less and Empower More

In a world where speed is profit, employees can't respond quickly to customer orders, special requests, and complaints if the rules require them to fill out forms in triplicate and get approval from several layers of management before acting. The solution is to flatten the traditional pyramid and give the people doing the work the authority to do whatever it takes (within reason) to make the customer happy right now.

Traditional layers of management and control served a useful purpose in earlier times. Before the era of computerized networks, information traveled much slower throughout the organization. The people at the top had little or no feedback about what was happening as it happened. To compensate for the dearth of information, layers of management were created to prevent departments and employees from spending too much or doing anything that might get the business in trouble. Slow growth and control were more important than innovation and service because uncontrolled growth and innovation had put many a company out of business before top management realized there was a problem. It's no wonder that bureaucracy is so stifling. That's what it's designed to do.

But information technology changed all the rules. Now it's possible for the CEO of a large, multinational company to electronically walk around every department of every factory, distribution center, and store every day and find out what's happening as it happens. If there is a problem, the information system calls it to his attention, and he takes steps to solve it before too much damage occurs. As a result, the need for layers of middle-management coordination and control become so much dead weight. If you're a middle manager working for a large company, whose job isn't directly involved with creating or selling a product or service, it may be time to consider a second career.

Rapid information shifts the priorities from slow growth and control to doing whatever it takes to make customers happy ASAP. Give people on the assembly line, front line, or wherever the latitude to bend the rules, make decisions and use their judgment to keep customers. Don't worry about their giving away the store. With the right information system, problems can be detected before serious damage is done. And failing to act quickly is far more costly in lost revenue from customers who never come back and tell others.

5. Develop Core Strengths and Partner More

Every human being has unique aptitudes. Success is achieved by discovering, developing, and using them. Joe Montana, Stephen King, Vladimir Horowitz, and Bob Hope all have unique talents. What they have in common is that each spends their time and energy concentrating on what they do best. The same is true for successful, flexible businesses.

Instead of trying to own and control every activity in the customer delivery chain, the agile business develops particular, unique strengths that will bring it the greatest long-term return. Essential activities better done by other businesses are carried out by forming ongoing, win-win partnerships.

The strategy of a traditional, vertically integrated company is independence and self-sufficiency. Business with suppliers and buyers is carried out at arm's length, often in an adversarial relationship.

On the other hand, the agile company strives for interdependence by teaming up with suppliers, retail outlets, or even competitors with complementary strengths. It finds partners and tells each one, "You do this, I'll do that, and we'll both benefit." This approach involves a lot of information sharing, trust, and the linking of electronic information systems across company boundaries. Needless to say, that's quite a break with tradition, but the payoff can be great. By concentrating on its strengths and letting partners do the rest, the agile company is less tied down by peripheral activities. Consequently, the business is less vulnerable to change and freer to move quickly into new markets.

For example, consider how Wal-Mart and Procter & Gamble are partnering for mutual benefit. In a traditional mode, Wal-Mart would order Pampers disposable diapers from P&G whenever inventory gets low. But under the partnership arrangement, Wal-Mart shares daily sales information with P&G, who continuously replenishes the stock as needed. Instead of ordering more Pampers periodically, Wal-Mart tells P&G, "We will tell you our inventory levels and you ship us more Pampers as needed."

Such an arrangement benefits both parties. Wal-Mart has increased its sale of P&G disposable diapers by 50 percent and cut inventory by 70 percent. Wal-Mart also benefits with higher customer satisfaction due to less chances of stockouts. The lower inventory costs enable Wal-Mart to offer everyday minimum pricing to its customers. It doesn't have to keep track of inventory levels and place orders because that job has been delegated to P&G. With continuous replenishment, Wal-Mart gets paid by the customers before they pay P&G. The Wal-Mart distribution system is so streamlined that goods only stay in the system for about five days before being sold, while P&G gets paid on a 15-day turn.

So what's in it for Procter & Gamble? Plenty. Like Wal-Mart, they benefit from increased sales and greater customer satisfaction. Fewer stockouts reduce the odds of the customer's changing brands. They also get valuable point-of-sale information every day on what's selling, which reduces the need to rely on sales forecasts. And because they know what's selling on a daily basis, P&G gets better factory utilization. Instead of the cycle of no orders, big order, no orders, the factory runs on a steady stream of output, producing according to the dictates of the retail customer. In this case, Wal-Mart's strength of rapid information gathering and distribution teams up with P&G's ability to deliver the goods on a continuous basis, and both benefit.

In another partnership agreement, General Electric helps small appliance stores compete with the big chains. In this arrangement, GE agrees to put appliances on display in the stores at no charge. When the customer orders an appliance, GE ships it within 24 hours. This is another arrangement where everybody wins. General Electric gets paid immediately and gains more retail outlets.

The small store isn't saddled with carrying inventory, and the customer gets the appliance quickly.

Quick-Response partnerships are taking the retail world by storm and three companies have teamed up successfully to make it work in the apparel area. In this case, the three players are Dillard Department Stores (the retailer), Warren Featherbone (the apparel manufacturer), and Milliken & Co. (the textile supplier). Warren Featherbone begins the process by bar coding its Alexis infants' wear and telling Dillard what the code stands for. The bar-code information is entered into the Dillard central computer.

When an Alexis item is sold at one of Dillard's 220 stores, the bar code is read and reported to the central computer. Every Saturday night Dillard generates weekly reorders based on sales information and forwards them to Warren Featherbone via electronic data interchange. Warren Featherbone receives the order on Monday morning, and within five days that order is ready. Dillard picks up the order with its own trucks. Using Quick Response, the lead time from Warren Featherbone to Dillard has been reduced from 45 to just 5 days. To keep the textile manufacturer up to date, Dillard also sends Milliken point-of-sale data via electronic data interchange. All three partners work in lock-step to keep the other supplied with what they need to give customers what they want, how they want it, when they want it.

Quick Response enables Dillard to offer customers a wide selection at low prices. Goods from over 400 of its suppliers are received in 12 days or less. And the payoff from Quick Response is handsome indeed. Dillard has enjoyed sales increases of 25 percent when those of comparable stores was 11 percent. Markdowns for targeted products are practically nonexistent. Dillard has also determined that a dollar invested in Quick Response is 16.3 percent more profitable than a non–Quick-Response dollar. And Warren Featherbone and Milliken benefit with valuable point-of-sale information, less need to rely on forecasting, lower inventory costs, and better factory utilization. Dillard's retail sales of Warren Featherbone products increased 34 percent in one year, while the average inventory relationship to sales remained unchanged. And Warren Featherbone was the very first Dillard supplier to ship products all 52 weeks of the year.

Rapid change and the need for agility have given birth to the era of partnering. Large companies such as General Electric and many others are increasingly giving more of their business to fewer suppliers in exchange for better prices, improved quality, information sharing, just-in-time deliveries, and a willingness to work together in joint problem-solving teams. Partnering reduces costs and increases quality, but it means working intensely with relatively few partners. Ron Yates of Jefferson Smurfit Corp, a major packaging supplier to large companies, summed up the partnering trend when he said, "Industrial salespeople are going to have to face the fact that we aren't going back to the old ways. If you don't follow your customers into partnering, then you'll be locked out— and your competitor will be the one doing the selling."

6. Technology Makes It Possible, Attitude Makes It Successful

It's your problem and your solution. It can be your greatest ally or your worst enemy. It can make you rich or put you out of business, and it may have already forced you to change careers. But like it or not, it has changed business forever and there's no going back. I'm referring, of course, to information technology.

Information technology makes it possible for giant companies to move like jack rabbits, and for small upstarts to compete with the giants. It's the great enabler that is offering incredible opportunities and profits for those who have learned to capitalize on it. Wal-Mart is a case in point. Its core capability of rapidly replenishing its stores wouldn't be possible without its massive investment in information technology. Similarly, Quick-Response partnerships, lean management, streamlined processes, and empowered employees are great concepts. But without the information technology in place to provide support and control, the results will be very disappointing, if not disastrous. The message to business in the future is clear: *Learn to harness the power of information technology and capitalize on it or go broke.*

But harnessing the power of information technology involves much more than buying the hardware and software and putting it to work. With new technology comes the need for an all-new mindset about how business is done. The new mindset focuses on time as the most important resource. Listening and responding to the customer replaces selling to the customer. Trying to do it all is supplanted by developing core capabilities and ongoing partnerships. Adversarial relationships with employees, suppliers, and customers are out and replaced with tearing down company walls, trust building, information sharing, and working together for mutual gain. And the process of getting things done is totally reorganized away from functional specialization and more toward continuously improving the process and working in teams to serve the customer. Discussing Quick-Response partnerships, Warren Featherbone President Charles "Gus" Whalen summed up the new attitude necessary when he said, "It forces companies to recognize the obvious—that people are interdependent."

7 | If It Doesn't Add Value, Don't Do It

Simplify and goods will flow like water.
—RICHARD J. SCHONBERGER

After battling the General Motors bureaucracy, H. Ross Perot, founder of Electronic Data Systems (EDS), remarked that the gunner's command at GM goes "Ready, aim, aim, aim, aim... At EDS," he continued, "the first person to see a snake kills it. At GM you put the snake in a box and organize a committee on snakes. Then you bring in a consultant who knows a lot about snakes. Next, you talk about it for a year. After a year, the snake hasn't bitten anybody so you let it back out on the floor."

The British scholar C. Northcote Parkinson is famous for his law that work expends to fill the time available. But one of his lesser-known laws is that early success leads to growth, and growth leads to size, which causes complexity, which inevitably leads to decay.

Painfully aware of this, businesses and organizations make across-the-board budget cuts, eliminate positions, and lay off employees in the hope that the operation becomes more efficient. But the results are usually less than hoped for because they don't begin by asking the right question. They ask, "How can we make this department, process, or job more efficient?" Instead, they should start by asking, "What's the worst that would happen if we

135

got rid of it completely or didn't do it at all?" If the consequences aren't catastrophic, get rid of it. Such behavior is consistent with the seventh commandment: If it doesn't add value, don't do it.

In today's highly competitive environment, every piece of equipment, every investment, every activity, and every job that doesn't add value is wasting time and money. Value is added by activities and resources that:

- Make the business more responsive to the customers, giving them more of what they need faster.
- Improve profits or quality.
- Free up previously tied-up resources, a new way of getting the same or better results with less money, less inventory, less people, or in less time.

Therefore, if you want to speed up your business, look at each activity and ask:

- Does this make us more responsive to our customers?
- Does it improve profits or quality?
- Does it make better use of resources?

If the answer to all three questions is no, don't do it, or get rid of it. That's the basic message of the seventh commandment.

DOWNSIZING: WHAT WENT WRONG

For over a decade, companies have been restructuring, downsizing, and trying to do whatever it takes to stay mean, lean, and competitive in a highly competitive, rapidly changing world. In the majority of cases, the results have been disappointing. A 1991 study by Wyatt Co., a Washington, D.C., management consultancy, surveyed 1,005 firms that had undergone major restructuring at least once. According to the Wyatt survey, only 46 percent of the firms met their expense-reduction goals, less than a third reached profit goals, and only 21 percent increased shareholder's return on investment. Another study by Mitchell & Company, a Massachusetts management consultancy, examined the impact of the 16 largest corporate restructurings carried out between 1982 and 1988. Again the results were disappointing. Three years after an announced restructuring, the typical firm's stock price trailed the competition by 26 percent. What went wrong?

Most downsizings went wrong because of the decision makers incorrectly defined the problem. They assumed delays, bottlenecks, and inefficiencies are caused by too many employees. Using that assumption, it follows that cutting employees increases efficiency.

But employees aren't the problem. Given an opportunity, they're the problem solvers. The problem is needless work, delays in the process, and outdated ways of getting things done.

The heart of any successful business is people and relationships. And when you start firing people, all sorts of unpleasant, unintended consequences follow.

First, downsizing damages morale and trust. Those who survive the cuts start feeling hostile toward the company. They begin to think, "Why bust your buns for a company who abandoned your friends and colleagues after years of devoted service? Maybe it's time to start looking for another place to work." Regardless of economic conditions, strong performers are always in demand and are likely to leave.

Second, the survivors get nervous. Instead of focusing on doing a good job, they begin to wonder if they're going to have a job. At a time when the company needs new ideas to work smarter, nervous people aren't going to suggest anything that might be the least bit risky. And God forbid they suggest a way to do their job more efficiently or eliminate unnecessary work. That could be economic suicide! They do everything strictly by the book, take little or no initiative, make sure they have written approval on all activities, and don't make waves. In short, nervous associates become card-carrying members of the CYA (Cover Your Ass) club.

A third problem is the legal consequences of layoffs. Almost anyone who is laid off can sue the company, claiming age, racial, or sexual discrimination. Employee lawsuits cost time, energy, money, can damage a company's reputation, and don't bring in a dime.

Finally, downsizing usually results in overworked survivors. The typical downsizing takes what has been called the "grenade approach." A fixed percentage of the jobs in an office or factory are blown out without changing the way work is done. Consequently, survivors are left to do their work and the work of their dismissed colleagues. A University of Michigan survey of white-collar downsizings in the auto industry found that survivors had to work 30 percent more hours just to keep up. And the Wyatt study found less than 37 percent of restructuring companies bothered to eliminate low-value work or increase automation to compensate for lost work. The result is employee burnout, unfinished work, and decreased quality.

In short, most downsizers incorrectly defined the problem, created more problems, and fired some of their best problem solvers. They violated the cardinal rule of restructuring:

CUT THE FAT, NOT THE PEOPLE

The people who do the job every day know the most about it. They know where the waste and the delays are. They can tell you what adds value and what doesn't. They have some of the best ideas for streamlining and simplifying. But if their livelihood is threatened, the chances of their cooperating are slim to none.

Employees aren't expenses to be trimmed. They are the most valuable source of continuous improvement.

Please don't misunderstand me. I'm not against dismissing people who don't do their jobs or who refuse to adapt to change. Nor am I against eliminating management, white-collar, and factory jobs when technology makes it possible to complete a task more efficiently with fewer people. That's progress, and I'm all for it. I also understand that today's economic realities make it difficult for businesses to offer iron-clad job security. But all too often a company responds to changing times with unemployment, when retraining and redeployment are better solutions.

Sea-Land Services provides an excellent example of a healthy approach to restructuring. Sea-Land realized in 1989 that it needed to become more customer responsive and less bureaucratic to compete with its Asian competitors in the containerized shipping industry. The goal was to improve reliability, reduce cycle times, and push decision making to the lowest possible levels of the organization. It concentrated on getting ideas from front-line employees, who work with customers every day. How can the customer be served better? What kinds of skills will people need to carry it out? And what kind of training will be needed?

Following eight months of information gathering and analysis, Sea-Land put its restructuring plan into action. Five layers of management and 800 positions were eliminated. Unnecessary work and redundant jobs were cut. Lengthy, obsolete job descriptions were updated and rewritten as succinct, one-page documents, focusing on the skills and abilities needed for each job. All employees were required to reapply and requalify for their jobs. One third of all employees and two thirds of exempt employees ended up changing jobs. And 400 people with no role to play in the new organization left. Instead of offering job security, Sea-Land offered employment security through training and development, and initial results are impressive. Two years after restructuring, shipping traffic was up 22 percent, revenues were up 32 percent, and employee bonuses were the largest in company history.

Most businesses overestimate the value of slashing payrolls and underestimate the negative impact of layoffs. A survey of manufacturers by the National Association of Accountants found that, on average, labor represents only 15 percent of the cost of making a product. Restructuring works best when its purpose is to cut response and cycle times, boost quality, and shrink inventories rather than to cut payrolls. Increasing agility has much more profit potential and fewer side effects than eliminating workers. Trying to downsize a business into prosperity is an exercise in futility.

FIND THE FAT AND CUT IT

The story goes that someone asked Michelangelo his secret for creating the sculpture of David. Michelangelo replied that there was no secret. The statue of David was already inside the stone. All he did was chip away the unnecessary parts. Similarly, inside every slow, sluggish, overweight business is a lean, agile one waiting to shed needless activities.

According to quality expert Armand Feigenbaum, "Forty percent of what we pay for in some products is for the waste imbedded in them." Here are five things you can do to help you find and remove the fat in your job, department, or business.

1. Talk to Your Customers

Begin by talking with your customers. What do they need from you? What can you do to improve quality or responsiveness in their eyes? Are you doing anything they find of little or no value? Are there any products or services that they have no use for? Finding answers to these questions is a good starting point for uncovering needless work. Any work that doesn't directly or indirectly provide some benefit to the customer needs to be cut.

It's also a good idea to identify your internal customers and get feedback from them. What do they need from you? What are you doing that's of no value to them? Are you doing anything that's keeping them from being of more value to the external customer? If so, it's got to go. Businesses prosper by creating value for the customer and go broke by creating busywork for those they employ.

2. Map the Process

Contrary to what you may believe, the fat isn't concentrated at the top or the bottom of organizations. It's marbled in throughout the entire business. A very useful tool for spotting and eliminating it is the process map.

A process map is simply a flow chart of every step taken in making or doing something. They can get rather elaborate and detailed, because every step, no matter how small, is listed on the chart. If an order comes in via telephone, picking up the phone is a step. If a signature is required, it's a step in the process and is listed on the chart. The best process maps are often put together by a team that includes employees, customers, and suppliers to verify that what the company thinks happens actually happens. It's common for process maps to take weeks to complete, and they can fill up conference room walls.

Having the entire process on paper makes it much easier to see the big picture and question the way things are done. Every step can be evaluated to see if it adds value. Suddenly, people start looking at previously unquestioned activities and steps and ask, "Why in the hell are we doing that? Let's get rid of it."

Process maps also help people come up with new ideas for

getting things done in less time. For example, General Electric's Evandale Ohio plant mapped the process of making turbine shafts for jet engines. The result was a 50 percent saving in time, a $4 million decrease in inventory and an increase in inventory turns from 2.6 to 7 per year. As General Electric CEO Jack Welch put it, "When you spend three days in a room with people mapping a process, the ideas just about bubble up inside. Just give them respect—everybody in the organization—and the improvement is enormous."

3. Eliminate Delays

It's amazing how the most obvious insights get overlooked. Some years ago, I went to the airport for my first flight on Southwest Airlines. Accustomed to flying on large airlines, I arrived at the gate about 25 minutes before flight time. The plane wasn't there. Fifteen minutes before flight time, the plane rolled up to the gate. For the next few minutes, arriving passengers got off. Then the passengers on my flight got on and we departed on schedule. When the flight arrived in Houston, we got off, other passengers got on, and the plane abruptly departed for another destination.

It appears that Southwest Airlines has discovered one of those very obvious but important insights: Airplanes don't make money sitting on the ground. Instead of sitting on the ground for hours, Southwest Airlines has a 15-minute turnaround time for its airplanes. This increases the revenue each plane earns and lowers the cost per passenger. It also allows Southwest to offer more flights per day, including 83 flights daily between Dallas and Houston. The enormous number of flights negates the need for an expensive computerized reservations system. Just go to the airport and Southwest will fly you there, in short order and for a very low price. Minimizing ground time and keeping the planes in the air is one key reason Southwest is prospering in an industry that has fallen on hard times. By minimizing delays in the system, they make better use of their assets, increase revenue, and lower costs.

Whether it's an office, a factory, a hospital, or an airline, delays tie up assets, cost money, and don't add value Simply eliminating needless delays can have an enormous impact on agility and the bottom line. As comedian Steven Wright remarked, "There's a fine line between fishing and standing on the shore like an idiot."

4. Simpler Is Better

According to author and professor Warren Bennis, "The factory of the future will have only two employees, a man and a dog. The man will be there to feed the dog. The dog will be there to keep the man from touching the equipment." It's an exaggeration but makes a good point. Where speed is important, simplicity is king. All other things being equal, less is more.

One key to Southwest Airlines' success is that it works hard to keep things simple. For example, the Southwest ticket doesn't look like the normal airline ticket. It looks more like a bus ticket or cash register receipt. When Southwest started flying outside the state of Texas, people were losing tickets, throwing them away, and running them through the family wash Just when they were about to spend multi-millions on a ticket system to issue routine airline tickets, one of their employees suggested, "Why don't we just print, in big capital letters, 'THIS IS A TICKET' on what we use now?" The problem was solved and millions of dollars were saved.

Another key to Southwest's low-cost strategy is that they fly only one type of airplane—the Boeing 737. The value here is that it minimizes training and inventory requirements and makes it much easier to substitute aircraft and reschedule pilots. Once again, less is more.

Anytime you can get down to one supplier to meet your needs, do it. You'll get a lower price and better quality and service by giving them all of the business.

Don't go on a technology buying binge before simplifying a process. It will only waste money and make things more complicated. Focus on improving customer service, reducing mistakes, and identifying unnecessary work and delays. Then consider the possibility of using technology to further simplify, speed up, or totally redesign the process. Make sure that your investment in technology is used to eliminate needless duplication, minimize delays, and get information to people who can act on it.

5. Cut the Red Tape

Is your company serving the customer or choking on red tape? Here's a test to help you find the answer. Call your company, posing as a customer with a problem. If the first person who answers the phone solves your problem or immediately directs your call to someone who can, you're in good shape. Otherwise, you probably have a bureaucracy problem. The more your call gets transferred, the worse it is.

Today's technology makes it possible to restructure work and retrain workers so that the one person having contact with the customer can help them solve their problems on the spot. That's what they did at First National Bank of Chicago's letter-of-credit department. Originally, customers who called the department were bounced from person to person when they called. The problem was the department's outdated assembly-line approach. A customer's request went through nine employees, dozens of steps, and took four days before a letter of credit was issued. The problem was solved by training each letter-of-credit issuer to handle every step of the process. Also, each customer deals with the same employee every time they order a letter. Computerized data bases make it possible for one issuer to have all the necessary information at their fingertips, which wasn't the case when the old method was designed. Under the new system, First Chicago issues letters of credit in less than a day at more than twice the volume, using 49 percent fewer employees.

But more often than not, getting rid of red tape consists of periodically examining and questioning every activity in the business, no matter how minute. Consider every job and procedure, every level of management and piece of paperwork, every step in a process and every expenditure, and ask those three key questions:

- Does this make us more responsive to our customers?
- Does it improve profits or quality?
- Does it make better use of resources?

When the answer is no, it's got to go.

8 | Build Teams, Not Empires

The age of the hierarchy is over.
—JAMES R. HOUGHTON,
CEO, Corning, Inc.

Bureaucracy isn't all bad; it played a major role in killing Soviet Communism. Unfortunately, it's doing the same thing to many of our business, governmental, health care, and educational institutions.

In business, the ground rules of bureaucracy go something like this:

Workers work and managers make decisions. Workers get things done and management gets things done through others. Divide your organization into functional specialties if you want it to be efficient. Create layers of managers and staff to coordinate and control all activities. Train everyone to do a narrow specialty. Let the marketers take care of the customers. Let the producers worry about quality and production deadlines. Leave the financial decisions to the bean counters.

It worked in simpler, less competitive times. For most businesses, those times are over.

In a world where speed wins, bureaucracy is just too slow. It's enormously expensive, usually takes forever to get things done, and results in watered-down decisions. Worse yet, decisions are usually made to benefit a particular bureaucrat or department, rather than the customer and the business as a whole. Whether you call them turf wars, chimneys, empires, or whatever, the result is the same. The bureaucrats become their own best customers. And that's no way to run a business.

Instead, we can tear down all those artificial walls between managers, workers, and functional departments. We can teach and equip workers with the skills and information they need to manage themselves. We can create new products and services by forming cross-functional work teams that work directly with customers and suppliers. And we can solve problems with multidisciplinary teams that make decisions in the best interest of the customer and the company.

Sound like pie in the sky? Well, companies such as Corning, 3M, Federal Express, and many others are speeding up their businesses by doing just that. It takes a different style of management, and it's not for everybody. But self-managed and cross-functional work teams are emerging as a terrific alternative to bureaucracies. Here are some of the many success stories being reported:

- A General Electric plant using teams to produce lighting panel boards increased productivity by 250 percent.
- A Federal Express team of clerks spotted and solved a billing problem that was costing the company $2.1 million per year.
- Using a team approach, Chaparral Steel has become the world's lowest-cost steel producer. It uses only 1.6 man-hours of labor to produce a ton of steel compared with 2.4 hours for other mini-mills and 4.9 hours for major producers.
- A 3M division using cross-functional work teams tripled the number of new products offered.

- Since organizing blue-collar workers into teams, Johnsonville Foods CEO Ralph Stayer estimates that productivity has risen at least 50 percent.
- A General Mills plant that opted for work teams reports productivity increases of up to 40 percent with no manager present on the night shift.
- Procter & Gamble, a work-team experimenter since the seventies, reports teamwork plants are 30 to 40 percent more productive than traditional facilities.
- By converting its insurance staff from a functional bureaucracy to work teams, Aid Association for Lutherans increased productivity 20 percent and reduced case-processing time by 75 percent.
- Using a team approach to product design, Chrysler developed its LH cars in record time, using half the number of people. And General Motors is reporting productivity gains of 20 to 40 percent at plants using team-based manufacturing systems.
- Shenandoah Life processes 50 percent more applications and customer service requests with 10 percent fewer people using work teams.

THE NEW MBA—MANAGEMENT BY ADULTERY

Sorry, but "management by adultery" isn't what you think it is. It's the term coined by Chaparral Steel to describe its management philosophy of treating workers like adults instead of children. And that, in a nutshell, describes the philosophical difference between the traditional and team approaches to organizing and assigning work.

The traditional approach has its philosophical roots in the industrial era, when workers were considered just another factor of production. Like machines, people were employed for their physical ability to produce. The underlying assumption is that workers are paid to work and not think. Thinking is management's job. The key to high productivity is to divide the work into small, specialized, repetitive, mindless tasks for all those workers who can't or don't want to think. In short, the traditional approach is management by direction and control. Whether they are aware of it or not, most large and many small businesses are organized on this philosophy. This philosophy gave birth to both the assembly line and the functional bureaucracy.

On the other hand, the team approach to organizing and assigning work grows out of an entirely different philosophy. Instead of viewing workers as just another factor of production, workers are seen as the key to production and continuous improvement. Instead of hiring people to do what management tells them, this approach assumes that the people who do the job are probably just as smart as management. Furthermore, inasmuch as workers do the job every day, they probably know the most about their job and have the best ideas for improving it.

So instead of hiring them to perform mindless jobs, *let's put their brains to work*. Treat them like responsible adults who know how to think and who want to do a good job. Instead of boring them with repetitive, narrow tasks, let's give them something challenging, meaningful, and important to do. Teach them the tools and techniques they can use to improve in their work and grow. Create a climate where they feel accepted and essential. And provide the rewards and recognition that make it worthwhile for them to go the extra mile and do great work. Instead of directing and controlling, this philosophy assumes that management's primary job is to create a climate where workers can contribute more and reward them when they do. In short, management's role in the new philosophy is to be less of a policeman and more of a motivator and coach. Instead of managing by direction and control, the new approach focuses on empowerment and self-control.

Meet the Self-directed Team

Self-directed work teams are the best and most natural response to this new philosophy. Every organization or group is a team because it consists of people interacting to achieve common goals. But self-directed teams have several distinguishing characteristics:

• Each team produces an entire product or delivers an entire segment of work to an internal or external customer.

• Team size varies from 3 to 30 members while the ideal size is 6 to 12.

• Members are highly trained and multi-skilled. It's common for everyone on the team to learn how to perform every job, and jobs are rotated among team members. This prevents boredom and increases team flexibility.

• Team members often come from various functional areas of expertise. For example, a product-development team might have members from production, marketing, finance, engineering, research, and development, and may include customers and suppliers. Team members learn from each other and can work more closely to increase customer satisfaction.

• They make their own management decisions. Depending on their stage of development, maturity, and autonomy, teams assume some, if not all, of the responsibility for managing and controlling themselves. Mature teams set their own goals, schedule and assign work, order supplies and equipment, hire, train and fire members, and determine member compensation and bonuses. Management's new job is to give them a mission, point them in the right direction, see that they get the necessary resources and feedback, encourage them, turn them loose, and get out of their way.

Why Are They So Effective?

As mentioned earlier, success stories of self-directed work teams typically report impressive payoffs in increased productivity and customer satisfaction. Here's why:

• *Teams are responsive, flexible, and agile.* While the traditional bureaucracy is like a rigid pyramid, the self-directed team is more like an octopus. It quickly swoops down on a problem or project, wraps its arms around it, makes decisions, and takes action. Members can be added to or taken off jobs as the situation dictates. The self-managed team is freed from the bonds of endless delays and approvals required in a rigid bureaucracy. Allowing members to use their own good judgment shortens or eliminates the time lag between spotting a problem and taking action to solve it.

• *Teams circumvent many of the problems of a functional organization.* Using cross-functional teams to design a new product (as discussed in Chapter 3) reduces the obstacles and problems of coordinating marketing, engineering, production, and financial decisions. Instead of each department's working on the problem in isolation and throwing it back and forth over departmental walls, experts from all areas work together to create what the customer wants and needs. The result is a better product, in less time, at a lower cost, using fewer people. For example, it took Chrysler 54 months and 2,000 technical staffers to design its K cars of the early eighties, using a traditional, functional approach to design. Employing work teams, the 1993 LH cars were designed in only 39 months with a technical staff of 740.

• *Teams foster pride and make work meaningful.* In one sense, self-directed teams restore the sense of satisfaction from work that was characteristic of the craft era that preceded the industrial revolution. When the shoemaker made a pair of shoes and the cabinetmaker built a cabinet, there was an accompanying feeling of deep satisfaction from seeing the results of hard work to complete a whole task. The craftsman could point to his finished work with pride and say, "I did that." Working in a narrow job on an assembly line or pushing paper in the bowels of a bureaucracy make it difficult, if not impossible, to get that kind of satisfaction from work. Self-directed teams tackle major projects and problems, and the work is structured so that every member's job is vital to the success of the team. As a result, everyone can point with pride to the results of the team and know that they were a meaningful contributor.

• *The social aspect of teams boosts worker satisfaction and commitment.* Instead of working in isolation on a narrow problem, members work together on an entire task, which most people find more satisfying. And working in teams increases commitment through positive peer pressure. The person who feels his job is crucial to the success of the team is more motivated to give his best than the person who feels like a small cog in a big wheel. The team is counting on him and he can't let them down.

But Will They Work Where You Work?

With work teams reporting 30 to 50 percent gains in productivity, it's easy to believe that they're the new panacea for ailing businesses. They aren't. Rather, teams are simply another way of organizing and assigning work. Also, it's important to remember that the companies reporting these successes didn't just reorganize into teams. They also invested heavily in training and new technologies, redesigned work processes, and made significant other efforts to improve quality and productivity.

Whether or not teams will work where you work depends largely on three factors: the nature of the work, the workers, and management. First, consider the nature of the business and the type of work. Is your business highly dependent on and organized around information? Are the jobs complex and interdependent? Are you faced with rapid, unpredictable change and increasingly demanding customers? Is there a need for faster decisions? The more yesses, the greater the likelihood that your business can benefit from work teams. Businesses in stable, predictable environments that require simple, repetitive jobs (like picking apples, planting seeds, or stuffing olives) aren't likely to benefit from work teams. But those types of businesses and jobs are growing fewer in number each year.

Second, take a good look at the workers. If their learning capabilities are severely limited, work teams aren't a good idea. Assuming they are capable of learning, are they willing to become more involved and take responsibility for making decisions? The plain fact is that some people just don't want to make decisions, think for themselves, or take any responsibility. If that describes the majority of the people where you work, the future isn't too bright for work teams. But more often than not, the reason people shy away from involvement and responsibility is because of the way they are managed. When management assumes that workers don't want to think or take responsibility, workers have an uncanny knack for living up to management's expectations. And a work climate where people are zapped for being wrong, and never rewarded for being right or showing initiative, isn't likely to see workers eagerly participating.

The third and perhaps most important factor to consider is if the democratic nature of work teams is compatible with the current style of management. If not, is management willing to invest the time, money, and pain that it's going to take to change the organizational culture? Teams do a whole lot more than change the way workers work. They change the very nature and role of managers, destroy bureaucracy, and flatten the organizational structure. Those who attained success by climbing the pyramid and exercising direction and control may not be overjoyed about relinquishing their authority and seeing the pyramid squashed. It's important for teams to have the support and commitment of management at all levels. One way to gain this commitment is to insure employment security for managers and point out that teams will free them from much of the drudgery of making daily, tactical decisions. The result is that they will have more time to concentrate on more important, strategic, long-term problems.

TEAM BUILDING ESSENTIALS

The movement toward team building is a clear and growing trend being dictated by the ever-increasing need for greater productivity, quality, and responsiveness. In the early eighties, about one employer in twenty utilized self-managed teams. By the early nineties, the number had grown to one in five with about seven to nine percent of all workers working on self-managed teams. Some experts estimate that by the turn of the century 40 to 50 percent of all U.S. workers will be members of self-managed teams.

While teams may be the wave of the future, creating successful, self-managed teams is a lengthy and involved process. As John Hanes, President of Effectiveness Dimensions, Inc., put it, "Teamwork used to be an option. But if you don't get on this bandwagon soon—realizing that it's going to take you three, five, even seven years to get there—you won't have the critical mass in the year 2000 to compete against organizations that are utilizing all of their talents."

While the concept of self-directed teams may be revolutionary, getting them up and running is evolutionary. Teams don't just form and start making autonomous decisions immediately. That's a blueprint for disaster. It takes time, training, and patience. As teams grow in competence and maturity, they are gradually given increasing authority to manage themselves. With that thought in mind, here are some key strategies and pitfalls to keep in mind when moving toward a team-based culture.

1. Start With a Steering Committee

Team building usually begins when someone at the top realizes that the old ways of organizing and assigning work just aren't working anymore. A new way has to be found to improve productivity, quality, and service or face losing customers, jobs, and eventually the business. Businesses, like individuals, are usually very resistant to change and aren't likely to opt for it unless there's much more pain involved in not changing.

Given the need, the first step toward creating teams begins with management's forming a steering committee, whose purpose is to champion and oversee the entire process of team development. In some organizations, the steering committee is composed of four to twelve members of top management from various functional areas. In other companies, members come from all levels of management, as well as union representatives, and future team leaders. Whatever the makeup, the steering committee's first task is to articulate a vision or mission statement of company values. For example, the mission statement at GM's Saturn operation is: "To market vehicles manufactured in the United States that are world leaders in quality, cost, and customer satisfaction through the integration of people, technology, and business systems, and to transfer knowledge, technology, and experience throughout General Motors."

Another key role of the steering committee is to investigate the feasibility of using work teams and recommend, or make a final decision, whether or not to employ them. Consultants and feasibility studies are very useful in this stage. Also, it's wise to have the steering committee visit one or more companies that are using work teams. There's no substitute for seeing the daily activities of a work team in person.

Assuming the decision is to go with teams, the steering committee appoints one or more design teams, whose role is to plan and direct the implementation strategy. While the steering committee's role is broad and strategic, the design team involves itself with the nitty-gritty details of forming, training and developing teams. Design teams usually consist of eight to fifteen members drawn from all levels and functional areas of management. It usually includes one or two members of the steering committee to insure good communication between both groups. And some design teams include union officials, functional experts (such as engineers or information systems specialists), and members of work teams.

Design teams determine such things as where teams will be used, who the members and team leaders will be, how they will be structured, what they will be responsible for, what training and support they will need, how team performance will be measured and rewarded, and how to make a smooth transition to work teams. Needless to say, it takes months of training, information gathering, and analysis before a design team is prepared to begin implementing teams. Like the steering committee, the design team is well served with the guidance of a seasoned consultant in team building and by making on-site visits to companies successfully using teams.

2. Train, Train, Train

Experienced practitioners in the art of team building unanimously agree that proper training is the single greatest key to successful teams. While the skills are numerous and varied, everyone from the top down needs to be oriented toward the team approach to getting things done.

Start at the top. Train managers first and cascade the training down the organization. Management needs training in how to become less of a director and more of an influencer or coach. A coach doesn't tell the team what to do. He gives them a mission, asks questions, and lets the team decide what to do. What was once a five-minute management decision may become a one-hour coaching exercise. To the manager involved, that may seem like an unnecessary waste of time. However, it's really an investment of time. As the team improves its decision-making skills, it will require less and less of the manager's time.

Work-team training usually includes three different types of skills:

• *Technical skills*. These are the unique skills needed to perform jobs assigned to the team. Learning how to operate machinery, maintain equipment, and process insurance claims or loan applications are examples of technical skills.

• *Human skills*. Becoming a team member increases the need for interpersonal competence. Members need training in how to work together, make decisions via consensus, resolve team conflicts, and provide constructive feedback. They need to learn how to provide motivation and support for each other. They need to learn how to negotiate with parties outside the team, such as other teams, management, customers, and suppliers. These are examples of human skills and they are crucial to building a successful team.

• *Administrative skills*. In order for a work team to become autonomous, members need to learn how to perform many of the duties previously done by management. How to schedule work, evaluate team and individual performance, prepare budgets, and read and interpret financial data are examples of administrative skills.

Companies that successfully employ work teams invest heavily in training. At its Blacksburg, Virginia, plant, Corning team members devoted 25 percent of all hours worked to training during the first year. Saturn requires team members to spend a minimum of 5 percent of their work time in training. Before production began at Saturn, all workers received from 300 to 700 hours of schooling. When Dana corporation switched its valve plant to teams, employees received 40 hours of training over 18 months. And Aid Association for Lutherans has a two-year training program that starts with individuals and progresses to intact teams.

With training requiring such a heavy investment, the key is to make sure it pays off. You don't teach every skill to every team, or overload members with more information than they can absorb in a given period of time. Determine the skills needed by each team, team leader, and level of management before beginning. To make sure the training sticks, teach a concept or skill to the members and then give them a problem or assignment where they can immediately apply what they learn.

3. Select the First Team Sites Carefully

As you probably suspect, the whole organization doesn't convert to teams overnight in most businesses. The more common way is to launch one or a few work teams, learn from the experience, and do what it takes to turn them into glowing successes. A successful start paves the way for slowly moving the rest of the company toward a team-based structure.

Choose initial team sites where the odds of success are high. Look for a place where management and workers are excited about the idea and want to give work teams a try. Look for a place where the people have a keen interest in learning and a history of high achievement. At the same time, you want a site that has high potential for improvement using teams. Look for a site that has a range of jobs that will enable team members to cross-train and learn multiple skills. And it's also important to look for a place where morale is good and people are already working well together. In short, give the initial teams every chance to succeed.

4. Be Alert and Prepared for the Stages of Team Development

It usually takes several years before a newly assigned work team becomes fully mature and capable of total self-management. In the process of maturing, teams pass through predictable stages of growth. They are:

• *Stage One—The Honeymoon*. Most members are optimistic and excited about the idea of working in teams. It's much like the honeymoon phase of a marriage. Hopes are high, but the parties have little or no idea of what they're getting themselves into. The team really isn't a team at this point. It's a collection of individuals. Heavy training is paramount in this stage, teaching members what they need to know to begin functioning as a team. The team also needs to understand its boundaries of authority, its main mission, and how it relates to the larger picture of serving the company and its customers. A team leader, usually not a member of management, is appointed to coordinate team activities and serve as a spokesperson for the team. In some organizations, the team leadership role is rotated among the members.

• *Stage Two—The Storm.* The honeymoon is over and the stress of learning new skills, roles, and relationships begins to take its toll. The team tends to flounder and shows signs of coming apart. Some members withdraw, while others form factions and rely only on those they trust. As management fades into the background, the team has to begin making decisions by consensus and finds reaching agreement very difficult.

While this stage appears counterproductive, the team is really starting to mature. Like an adolescent, the team will experience conflict and chaos as the first steps toward becoming a cohesive group. Management's job is to forewarn the team that this will happen and equip them with the communication- and conflict-resolution skills to get them through this stage. The worst thing management can do is step in and start directly resolving conflicts for the team. During the storm, it's important for management to remain positive, stress the importance of staying the course, and remind the team that this difficult period won't last forever.

• *Stage Three—The Tight-knit Team.* As the storm subsides, the team becomes a true team. It knows its role, what it has to do, and how to do it. Members are like the Three Musketeers—all for one and one for all. Loyalty to the team and its mission are paramount in the minds of the members.

The danger in this stage is that the team may become so dedicated to itself that it neglects its role as a part of the larger organization. It may view management, customers, suppliers, or other teams as adversaries to be opposed rather than groups to be served. To counter this tendency, training needs to focus on the need to communicate and work with those outside the team. Getting customer feedback, working with suppliers, and communicating with other teams are important activities to stress in this stage.

• *Stage Four—The Self-managed Team*. It usually takes at least two years from inception to reach this final stage. Now the team manages itself superbly with little help from management. It makes decisions based on the overall strategic interests of the business. It understands the importance of serving both internal and external customers, making a profit for the business, and serving the larger community.

Once this stage is reached, management's main role is to make sure the team doesn't regress into earlier stages. Continuous training and support are essential to allow the team to improve its skills and grow. Opportunities are provided for the team to work in partnership with other teams, suppliers, and customers. When management makes important decisions affecting the team, it gets the team's input. Management spends time working with and encouraging teams without making decisions for them. And teams are thoroughly recognized and rewarded for doing outstanding work.

5. Reward Teams, Not Stars

We live in a culture that worships individual achievement. Who won the Heisman trophy? Who was valedictorian? Who was voted most valuable player? Who is the top salesman? Who is employee of the month? Who won the Miss America pageant? Recognizing and rewarding individual achievement is a great idea—when you want outstanding, individual achievement. When you want stars, reward stars.

However, with work teams, the teams are the stars. Therefore, it's important that any rewards or recognition be based on team performance rather than individual performance. If you find team members not cooperating, check the reward system where you work. Are people rewarded for individual performance? How are raises, bonuses, promotions, titles, and other perks determined? In most organizations, the system is set up to reward individual achievement. For teams to flourish, the entire team needs to share in the rewards of outstanding team performance. A business that asks for teamwork and rewards individual performance is sending the troops a mixed message.

This doesn't mean that everyone on the team needs to be rewarded equally. That's a decision that's best left up to the team. For example, one common way to reward teams is through gain sharing or profit sharing. A product-development team might have an agreement where they receive ten percent of a new product's profits after the development costs are recovered. How should the gains be distributed among the team? Does every member of the team receive an equal share? Let the members decide. Also, when it comes time to evaluate team members for merit increases or bonuses, use peer evaluations. Ask members to rate themselves and others in terms of how much each contributed to the team. Peer evaluations are usually an accurate measure of a member's contribution and serve as a good motivational tool. Knowing those we work with every day will be evaluating us tends to keep us on our toes.

One effective way you can reward team members as individuals is through a pay-for-knowledge program. With pay-for-knowledge, a team member increases their base pay by mastering a body of knowledge or particular skill that makes them more valuable to the team and the company. (More about this in Chapter 9.)

Finally, when a system is set up to reward teams, make sure it's a system that doesn't reward one team at the expense of another. Just as it's desirable to reduce competition within each team, it's just as important to have harmony and cooperation between teams. Ideally, you want everybody's competitive energies focused on winning and keeping customers in the marketplace, where there's plenty of competition.

6. Turn Them Loose Gradually

If self-directed teams are empowered to make decisions once made by management, the obvious question is, "Which decisions?" The answer depends primarily on the team and its stage of growth. Empowerment isn't like a college degree that you either have or don't have. Rather, it's a matter of how much.

Teams need to be empowered gradually. Begin by delegating decisions that are challenging but within their capabilities. As they master one set of responsibilities, train them to assume additional duties and delegate.

For example, in the early stages of team development, learning is paramount, and the team assumes little responsibility. Initially, team decisions are limited to activities such as housekeeping chores, training each other, and maintaining and repairing equipment. As they demonstrate proficiency in making good decisions, more authority is delegated. The team is empowered to do their own scheduling, find and solve their own quality problems, meet with customers, and order supplies. With further maturity, even more latitude is given to the team to control their own work and environment. They hire team members, prepare budgets, design their own work layout, and make equipment-purchasing decisions. Finally, at the most mature level, teams make virtually all decisions within their boundaries. They measure and appraise their own performance, discipline each other, and make their own compensation decisions. But to reach this level usually takes years of training and trial and error.

One useful exercise is to make two lists at the outset. On one list put all the responsibilities of the team. On the other list, write down all the initial responsibilities of management. As the team progresses and matures, activities can be transferred from the management list to the team list. In addition to clarifying who's accountable for what, this exercise serves as a useful feedback tool. As more duties are delegated to the team, the team list becomes a scorecard for growth and development.

7. The Middle Management and Supervisory Transition Is Crucial

There's no denying the fact that team building means fewer layers of management and fewer managers. Those in top management relish the thought of not having to deal with an unwieldy bureaucracy. Those on teams like the idea of having more control and doing more satisfying work. But those in supervisory and middle-management positions worry about losing their status and their jobs. Yet a successful transition to work teams is difficult, if not impossible, without the support and commitment of supervisors and middle managers. The problem: How do you get these two groups to commit themselves to the demise of their own positions? It's almost like asking someone to plan their own funeral.

The first and most important thing is to make it clear that opportunities for employment, meaningful work, and rewards will be available to all who are willing to commit themselves to team building. Teams require fewer managers. But it doesn't necessarily mean that fewer people are needed. Indeed, displaced managers have much to contribute. Their experience, insights, and ideas can help build better, stronger teams. Point out that creating a more productive organization is the key to employment security and better pay.

As for status, it's only normal for some managers and supervisors to have their egos bruised when they cease to be in positions of direct authority. One way to soften the blow is to let them keep their old titles. At the same time, assign them a second title that accurately depicts their role in the new structure. Keeping the old title lets them save face. They won't have to explain to their family and friends that they weren't demoted in the restructuring. As they retire or leave the company, the old title can be phased out.

At the same time it may be useful to establish new ladders of nonmanagerial titles for people to climb. These new titles can reflect someone's value and contribution to the company rather than a level of management. For example, universities promote faculty members from Instructor to Assistant Professor to Associate Professor to Professor, to reflect their contribution and value to the university. While their pay and title increase, their role in the organization basically remains the same. With fewer opportunities in management, different avenues of rank and compensation will be needed to reflect someone's growth and value to the business.

But what are all these former managers and supervisors going to actually do? As it turns out, there are several options available. Those with good communication skills can be reassigned as facilitators to help teams communicate both internally and with the rest of the organization. They sit in on team meetings, train team members, help teams work through problem-solving processes, and work with other teams.

Those with a strong knowledge of a particular product or process can be reassigned as technical experts. They can help teams solve problems and suggest ideas for continuous improvement.

Still others can serve as transitional supervisors, who work with teams in the early stages of transition. Others can become area managers, whose role is to coordinate efforts between teams and the larger organization. And still others, who are secure in themselves and enjoy hands-on work, can opt to become team members.

Unfortunately, some will find the new structure intolerable and seek employment elsewhere. While that may seem unfortunate, it's ultimately for the best. Success, more than ever, requires working with those who are willing to change. The on-going need to adapt and adjust to new roles, responsibilities, and duties is a major requirement in the new world of business.

9 | Lifelong Learning Is Everybody's Job

> *In a time of drastic change, it is the learners who will inherit the future.*
>
> —ERIC HOFFER

A few years back I had the pleasure of meeting Bob Burnett when he was Chairman of the Board of Meredith Corporation, the parent company of *Better Homes and Gardens, Ladies Home Journal* and numerous other excellent magazines. Bob enjoyed a very long and successful career at Meredith and it's hard to imagine anyone being more admired and respected by his associates. One evening at dinner I asked him, "What's the biggest difference between the Meredith Corporation you joined as a young man and Meredith today?"

"Two things," Bob replied. "First is the tremendous amount of change that we face every day. And second, because of the change I feel like I'm running as much of an educational institution as a business."

Traditionally we have separated the world of learning from the world of work. The schools cooked you until you were done and then you went to work. But like many ideas, this one has lost all relevance. Today you have to be continuously cooking. Any business, department, work group, or individual that isn't continuously learning new and better ways to do the job is going to get

166

steamrolled by the competition. The old adage, "If you think education is expensive, try ignorance," is truer today than ever. Ignorance is not bliss. It's bankruptcy.

There's good news and bad news when it comes to learning. The good news is that it's in high demand and pays better than ever. During the eighties, the average wage of a 24–34-year-old college-educated male increased ten percent after inflation, while incomes of high-school graduates dropped nine percent. A college-educated male earns almost twice as much today as a high-school graduate, and the gap is widening. From a global perspective, *Business Week* magazine painted an accurate picture of the new economy that affects us all: "Competitive advantage no longer belongs to the biggest or those blessed with abundant natural resources. In the global economy, knowledge is king. And those nations that excel in creating new knowledge and transforming it into new technologies and products will prosper in years to come."

The bad news is that the U.S. labor force is teeming with tens of millions of people who haven't learned how to learn. Between 23 and 27 million American adults are classified as functionally illiterate; they can't read a newspaper or fill out a job application form. Another 12 million are marginally better, but lack the basic skills to perform necessary tasks in a modern factory. That's an enormous waste of human potential when you consider that the total U.S. labor force is 117 million.

Somewhere along the line, schools, students, and parents fell down on the job. And now woefully unprepared people are looking for work in a knowledge-intensive, information-oriented, rapidly changing, global economy. It's a big problem for people who need work and for businesses who need skilled people. As author and economist Lester Thurow put it, "If Japan can graduate 96 percent of its high-school students, we can't allow one-third of American high-school students to drop out. In a global economy you may live in a first-world country, but if you get a third-world education, then eventually you will get third-world wages." Between 1979 and 1992, real wages for high-school dropouts fell 20 percent.

Fixing the schools and lowering the drop-out rate are the long-term solutions. But businesses can't wait for the schools to improve. They need skilled people now. And the person without a job or whose job is threatened can't simply shrug his shoulders and say, "Too bad I didn't learn about that in school." He needs job skills now.

The immediate answer to the problem is twofold. First, businesses need to invest in equipping employees with the necessary learning and job skills. And second, everyone who wants to grow and prosper must take personal responsibility for learning the latest skills and techniques in their field. In the final analysis, we're all in business for ourselves. And staying up to speed means staying up to date through lifelong learning.

LEARNING ON THE JOB

According to an old Chinese proverb, "If you want one year of prosperity, grow grain. If you want ten years of prosperity, grow trees. If you want one hundred years of prosperity, grow people." While U.S. corporations spend between $30 billion and $40 billion a year on corporate training and development, only 1 out of every 14 workers has ever received any formal training from an employer. Instead, most of the training budget goes to sales, professional, and management development programs. While these programs are vital, they just aren't enough. If the United States is to remain a first-rate economic power, it's essential that we focus more resources on training and educating the 76 percent of all workers who don't have college degrees.

Fortunately, some companies such as Corning, Motorola, and others are leading the way with grass-roots training and educational programs, proving that Ben Franklin's advice is more true today than ever: "An investment in knowledge pays the best interest." According to the American Society for Training and Development (ASTD), every $1 invested in training and education generates $3 in economic activity. And Motorola estimates that every dollar it spends on training generates $30 in productivity gains within three years.

Before we look at several approaches to on-the-job learning, two points need to be made. First, workplace learning is not an exercise in altruism or social responsibility for most businesses. It's a business investment whose purpose is to make those who work for the business more productive. Any plan to implement job-related learning begins by focusing on customers. Look at every person in every job and answer the following question: "What will this person have to know to exceed our customers' expectations?" If a customer calls with a special request or complaint, what type of equipment and training will it take to have the first person who answers the telephone solve his problem? What types of skills will our factory workers need to produce the kinds of products that win and keep customers? Effective workplace learning makes the business more valuable to the customer by making the learner more valuable to the business.

Second, we need to distinguish between training and education. Training is teaching someone how to perform a specific task, such as operate a piece of machinery, work a switchboard, or process an insurance claim. A person can be trained to perform all the steps of a task without knowing or caring why any of them are important. On the other hand, education involves learning much more than what to do. It's an ongoing process that hopes to improve understanding, causes people to question the status quo, and makes improvements. Training teaches us to follow a prescribed course of action. Education teaches us to think for ourselves. Computers and robots can be "trained" to perform mindless routines better, faster, and cheaper than humans. While it's important to teach people specific skills, the new economy requires people who know how to think clearly, critically, and creatively. Education is the wellspring for continuous improvement.

Let's look at several types of programs having positive payoffs for both the businesses and their workers, beginning with the most basic of all.

Workplace Literacy

There was a time when factory jobs were so repetitive, narrow, and specialized that performing them was basically a no-brainer. Since most jobs didn't require basic learning skills, many workers didn't have them. Then high technology and global competition changed all the rules.

Today's workers have to learn how to operate, maintain, and understand sophisticated equipment. They have to learn how to communicate and work together in teams to solve problems and be prepared to master even more sophisticated manufacturing techniques in the future. And that's an impossible assignment when you can't read, write, or do basic calculations.

In the late seventies, Motorola discovered that many of their workers couldn't read or do simple arithmetic. To correct the problem, Motorola declared that all employees must have seventh-grade-level communications and computational skills, which would soon be raised to eighth- and ninth-grade levels. But this created a huge problem. How do you motivate people with 20 or more years on the job to learn basic skills? It's embarrassing to admit illiteracy. And many of these people feared the idea of schooling because they failed at it in their youth.

Motorola solved the problem by requiring all employees, regardless of educational level or position in the company, to take regular retraining to upgrade their skills. If people failed retraining, they wouldn't be fired. Motorola would find a way to help them succeed. However, anyone who refused training would be fired. When 17 people who refused training were dismissed, the word was out.

Not surprisingly, companies that help workers learn the three R's report that they perform their jobs quicker and more efficiently. And sometimes the innovative payoff is awesome. Jerry Sanders worked for General Motors Delco Remy factory in Anderson, Indiana, for 29 years without knowing how to read, write, or count. After learning the three R's through GM's workplace learning, he devised a way for equipment costing only $75,000 to perform a job that previously required equipment costing over $1 million. According to Sanders, learning the basics made it possible. In the same plant, after learning to read and write, Terry Henderson, along with two coworkers, came up with a way to improve machines so that shafts made for starter motors came out straight instead of crooked. Each man received an award payment of $2,000 from GM.

In addition to boosting productivity and innovation, basic-skills training improves morale and company loyalty. In addition to getting a paycheck, workers are gaining vital skills to lead a more productive and satisfying life. And it gives the learners a significant ego boost.

If you are considering implementing a basic-skills program where you work, there's help available from community colleges and adult-education institutions. Visit the ones in your area to find out what types of programs are available. Ask about sources of state and local funding to help defray the cost. Ask if they can hold classes at work. Ask about computer-assisted learning programs where people can progress at their own pace. Ask how to screen workers to determine what skills they need. Ask about ways to teach the skills in a motivating and nonembarrassing way. And speaking of motivation, here's an increasingly popular approach being used to boost interest in learning new job skills.

Pay-for-Knowledge

The basic idea is simple. Instead of paying people by the hour, rank, or seniority, base part of their pay on the number of job-related skills they master. Most companies and workers who have tried it like it because it benefits both parties. The benefits to the company are:

- *Increased flexibility*—The more jobs workers can do, the easier it is for the business to adapt to changing market conditions, work flows, and crises.
- *Improved customer service*—The more jobs a person on the front-line can perform, the greater the odds of their being able to solve a customer's problem on the spot.
- *A leaner, lower cost organization*—Companies with multi-skilled people find they can get more done with fewer people.
- *Higher morale and commitment*—Multiskilled workers are less likely to be bored and more likely to see the broader picture of how what they do is important. They feel more involved, which improves morale and reduces absenteeism and turnover.
- *Higher productivity*—The more a worker knows how to do, the more she can do. Improved productivity is almost guaranteed.
- *Higher Quality*—The more skilled a person is, the greater the odds of his doing the job right the first time.

The obvious benefit to employees is more money. Workers typically make 10 to 20 percent more than they would have under a more traditional system. Pay-for-knowledge also provides a way for employees to measure their growth, other than climbing up the organization, at a time when pyramids are being flattened. Finally, the improved morale, opportunity to be of greater value, and do more meaningful work are psychic rewards.

Not surprisingly, you tend to find pay-for-knowledge programs where you find self-directed work teams. But how companies certify skills competency and pay-for-knowledge vary greatly from company to company. Here are several examples:

Shenandoah Life Insurance Co. of Roanoke, Virginia, identified 144 different skills required of workers and estimated how many weeks it takes to master each skill. Learning all 144 skills takes an estimated 321 weeks. The easiest take one week and the most difficult take sixteen weeks to master. Employees learn a new skill from team members, and team members certify when the worker has mastered a given skill. A worker's pay is determined by how many hours of skills he has mastered. For example, let's assume the lowest-paid worker makes $900 per month, and the highest pay a worker can make is $2,000 per month. The differential is $2,000 minus $900 or $1,100. A person who had mastered 150 weeks of skills would have earned $150/321$ or 46.73 percent of the potential number of hours. Therefore his pay would be $900 plus 46.73 percent of $1,100 or $1,414.03 per month.

On the other hand, Embassy Suites uses an entirely different approach. Hotel employees who want to cross-train for a new skill must complete 480 hours working in a new position and pass a written exam with a minimum score of 90 percent. The pay is a one-time bonus of $300.

In their pay-for-performance/pay-for-knowledge system, Federal Express uses video disc instructions and job-knowledge testing to improve the skills and pay of its front-line people. The video disc allows workers to work at their own pace, learning standardized instructions on product knowledge, and various aspects of their jobs. Every six months, workers take a two-hour test, and test scores count for 12 percent of their six-month review. Excellent test scores improve the odds of securing raises and promotions.

AT&T Credit Corporation's pay-for-knowledge program requires workers to take a half-hour exam, be evaluated by other team members, and meet the requirements of a six-month performance agreement before being certified for a new skill. Being certified earns an average raise of $1,400 per year.

The diversity of these approaches illustrates an important point. Any pay-for-knowledge program needs to be customized to meet the needs of a particular business and will likely need to be modified, updated, and improved over time. But if knowledge and lifelong learning are important where you work, consider pay-for-knowledge. What a company is willing to pay for tells those who work for the company what's really important.

Self-directed Learning

Traditional classroom training and education can be very expensive. It can also be very ineffective, because everyone learns at a different speed and instructional quality varies. And it can also be very boring, because not all instructors are created with equal enthusiasm and delivery skills. But today it's possible to receive some of the finest quality training and education and learn it at your own pace. Just as technology is creating the need for lifelong learning, it's also giving us the tools to improve the efficiency and effectiveness of learning.

The marriage of computer, CD-ROM (compact disc—read only memory), and television technology has created a medium called interactive video disc (IVD) that lends itself well to learning. With IVD, a student sits at a computer terminal and learns information played on a video disc. The program also quizzes the student on what he's learned and provides feedback and test scores. IVD learning has several excellent benefits:

- Everyone receives the exact same training content in the exact same manner.
- Each person can progress at their own pace and skip over material they already know.
- Employees can learn when they have the time and don't have to wait for a scheduled class.
- They get immediate feedback on their progress.
- They can go back and review any topics as much as they wish.
- New skills can be learned and old ones can be updated simply by sending out information via telephone to disc players anywhere in the world.
- It requires only about one-third as much time as traditional classroom learning to achieve the same results.
- Finally, the cost savings can be enormous. Federal Express estimates that using IVD technology to provide quality training for its 75,000 U.S. employees represents a savings of 80 percent over the cost of conventional classroom training.

When it comes to teaching technical skills, self-directed learning makes a lot of sense. The Learning Curve is the name of the self-directed learning center opened by office equipment manufacturer Steelcase, Inc., in Grand Rapids, Michigan. Trainees use videotapes, audio tapes, interactive video discs, computerized tutorials, and workbooks to learn word processing, spreadsheets, data-base management, project management, and other topics. The twelve-workstation facility was completed in nine months for a total cost of $80,000. That's 20 percent less than they were paying an outside firm to deliver computer-based training.

Sausage-maker Johnsonville Foods takes a very liberal approach to self-directed learning. Some years ago the focus of the company was changed from using people to build a great business to using the business to build great people. As a result, the training department became the member-development department. Instead of training, the new purpose of the department became the mental development of its members. Each member has a $100 fund set aside each year to devote to any development activity of their choosing. It doesn't have to be job related. It just has to be a learning activity that will encourage the person to think. Johnsonville also keeps a mini-library of books, audio and video tapes, and magazines of interest to members. Personal-development workshops are held to help members gain greater self-awareness. Morale, profits, and productivity have all soared under this new approach.

BUSINESS/EDUCATION PARTNERSHIPS
A WINNING COMBINATION

As I mentioned earlier, business and educational institutions have traditionally lived and worked in separate worlds. Professors refer to life outside the ivory tower as life in "the real world." But today, business and education need each other more than ever. Both worlds need to tear down the walls between them and form working partnerships for mutual gain. Today's "real world" requires educators who will treat business as a valuable customer, who buys their products and services. And businesses need to treat educators as suppliers of some of their most precious resources— skilled people, knowledge, development, and innovation.

Actually a successful business/education partnership is very similar to any business/supplier partnership. It's an ongoing, win-win relationship. It requires a lot of information sharing so that each party understands the needs of the other. The company works with a limited number of schools in exchange for giving them a lot of business. And in return for their business, the school provides the company with the students, skills training, development, and innovation according to the company's quality specifications. Here are some ways that businesses and schools are partnering for mutual gain:

Youth Apprenticeships

The American educational system has only two tracks: college prep and nowhere prep. A high-school diploma has become virtually unmarketable. Furthermore, a college degree is no longer a guaranteed passport to success. Evidence is mounting that the U.S. is creating more college graduates than jobs for them. We need to do a better job of preparing young people to make a successful transition from school to work.

One possible solution that's gaining momentum is the youth apprenticeship program, where students train, mostly on the job, for a skilled occupation of their choosing. Germany uses such a program with great success. Nearly 70 percent of all 15- to 19-year-old West Germans train for their livelihoods in youth apprenticeships. They typically spend three or four days a week working with a mentor in a business, and one or two days in class learning the necessary academic skills. Students can choose from almost 400 skilled occupations in fields as diverse as manufacturing, health care, banking, computer technology, and many others. National standards are set in every occupation, and apprentices must pass certifying examinations in order to qualify for entry into their field. Once the apprenticeship is completed and the student is certified, they may be hired by the company who trained them or go to work elsewhere.

Students benefit from apprenticeships because they get a career head start and are paid while learning. They develop good work habits and learn how to work with others, and their classroom learning becomes more relevant. A student who applies what he learns in class today on the job tomorrow is more motivated to study.

The businesses benefit too. Apprentices are an inexpensive source of skilled labor. Additionally, the company gets a firsthand look at potential employees and can pick the best talent.

While not nearly as organized or extensive as Germany, there are signs that apprenticeships are growing in popularity in the U. S. Sears has established a pilot apprenticeship program where 17-year-olds are learning to be appliance repairmen. In Boston hospitals, apprenticeship programs are training students in sophisticated fields such as radiology and nuclear medicine. And in Charleston, Robert Bosch Corp., a German manufacturer, has established an apprenticeship program to train South Carolina youths to make auto parts. With so many people needing job skills and so many companies needing skilled people, the apprenticeship movement can only grow.

Retraining Workers Through Cooperative Education

What's going to happen to all of the displaced factory and office workers whose jobs have been eliminated?

One promising answer lies in the establishment of cooperative education programs between technical schools and local businesses. In a co-op program, students usually alternate between being full-time students and full-time employees. For example, Mary goes to school for the fall semester studying to be a laboratory technician and spends the spring working in a local hospital lab. Most programs run from two to four years.

Many of the same benefits of apprenticeships are found in cooperative education programs. Businesses get a source of inexpensive labor and a firsthand look at potential employees. And students gain on-the-job experience and a paid job while learning a new livelihood.

The key to making cooperative education successful is to make it a true partnership between the schools. the students, and local businesses. One of the most successful examples can be found in Cincinnati, Ohio, where five institutions offer such programs. The schools work closely with businesses to make sure that they turn out graduates in fields where local jobs are available. Course content and curricula are regularly modified to meet the needs of the job market. Night classes are held to accommodate work schedules, and child-care facilities are available for students having children. And the payoff from such a partnership is handsome indeed. Cincinnati Technical College. a two-year state school, finds skilled jobs for 98 percent of its co-op students.

Customized Course Offerings

When Corning decided to upgrade worker educational and skills training, the training department faced an enormous assignment. The department felt it should be concentrating its efforts on high-impact programs that would drive long-run change, such as team-building skills, innovation, and managing diversity. They decided to farm out all training aimed at individual employees. This was carried out in a partnership with the College Center of the Finger Lakes (CCFL), a nonprofit institution that offers college-level courses in the Corning. New York area.

In the partnership, CCFL offered 60 courses previously taught by Corning, such as financial accounting, statistical process control, selling, and customer service skills. The benefit to Corning was that the training department was now free from routine skills training and able to concentrate on the high-impact programs with greater long-range payoffs. And the payoff to CCFL was a significant increase in revenue.

One reason the partnership proved successful was that it was a true partnership. Each department of Corning paid CCFL for the training of its employees just as they had paid the training department in the past. New courses were developed for Corning as needed. Employees registered for courses and attended them just as before. And Corning shared its mainframe computer, corporate billing system, training staff meetings, and other facets of internal communication with CCFL as if it were a part of the company. By blurring the boundaries between organizations, both worked together for mutual gain.

Mutual Exchange for Mutual Benefit

Similarly, much of Motorola's success in training and education comes from treating its educational suppliers like partners. Regular meetings are held every few weeks between Motorola executives and deans, professors, college presidents, principals, and teachers to discuss the needs of both parties. Through this dialogue with educational institutions ranging from elementary schools to graduate schools, Motorola learns what skills are being taught. And the educators learn what skills need to be taught in order to survive and prosper in an increasingly competitive global economy.

But the exchanges don't stop there. In addition to supplying tuition and sending them thousands of students each year, Motorola regularly donates equipment to community colleges. Motorola also provides summer internships and in-house training slots for community college faculty. Faculty are encouraged to visit their plants, learn about state-of-the-art manufacturing, and use their lab equipment to teach all of their students. Motorola sponsors a planning institute for superintendents from 52 school districts in 18 states on how to formulate strategic educational plans and work with businesses. At the university level, Motorola and Northwestern jointly designed a quality course for Northwestern's MBA program. Northwestern offers courses taught jointly by a professor and a Motorola expert. These are just a few of many ways that Motorola U. (the name given to Motorola's giant educational and training effort) is successfully teaming up with educators in a win-win partnership.

Using Knowledge and Innovation to Spur Economic Growth

Much has been written and said about the Japanese economic miracle of the last several decades. In a relatively short time, Japan, with an educated work force, hard work, and meager natural resources, literally went from ground zero to become the world's second largest economic power. Much of the success is attributable to what has been called Japan, Inc. It's a co-ordinated effort in which the government, the banks, and businesses worked together in a partnership to build Japan's prosperity around key industries, such as steel, automobiles, and electronics. Everyone worked together in a coordinated plan. And the plan worked.

Similarly, coordinated partnerships between businesses, educational institutions, state and local governments, and venture capitalists are springing up in various areas of the U. S. and creating regions of hot economic growth. At the heart of most of these economic hot spots lies one or more major research universities. They produce graduates, knowledge, and technologies for new products. The government provides financial support for education and a climate to attract established businesses and encourage the creation of new ones. The venture capitalists provide seed money to start new businesses, which turn the technologies into marketable products. And the businesses create jobs and prosperity for the area. The Silicon Valley of California, Research Triangle of North Carolina, and Boston's Route 128 were the first areas to spawn new businesses as a result of their proximity to major universities.

Meanwhile, other regions of the country learned from high-tech success stories like the Silicon Valley and went to work. In Texas, businesses, along with state and local governments and the University of Texas, built up Austin's high-tech industry. Major high-tech businesses were courted and encouraged to locate around Austin. The university was well funded and financing was secured for promising new businesses. The result of this effort is the creation of Silicon Hills, a high-tech corridor of 450 companies and 55,000 jobs making computers and computer chips. Similarly, Medical Alley of Minneapolis houses 500 health-care related companies and provides 40,000 jobs. And Princeton Corridor houses 400 companies providing over 130,000 jobs in the biotech and telecommunications fields.

Not all economic growth needs to be research based. The ability and willingness to provide a solid, well-trained labor force can have a huge impact. That's one reason that BMW chose Spartenburg, South Carolina, over 250 other potential sites as the place to locate a new manufacturing plant. In exchange for coming to Spartenburg, the state of South Carolina agreed to provide a comprehensive preemployment worker training program. The state agreed to handle recruiting, testing, and screening of potential employees. It agreed to build an on-site educational facility for the exclusive use of BMW. It agreed to hire qualified instructors, and provide tools, manuals, and classroom facilities and extensive high-quality training customized to BMW's needs. Workers will receive training in technical skills and teambuilding, and there will be apprenticeship programs as well. That may sound like an expensive commitment, and it is. But it's estimated that in a ten-year period, the BMW facility will pour over $6 billion into South Carolina. That's 150 times the amount that South Carolina will invest in educating and training.

In summary, business/education partnerships have a major and growing role to play in a world where change is the status quo. Some educators are very antibusiness. I wonder who they think creates the wealth to pay their salaries. And some business people see academics and educators as impractical idealists with little or nothing to offer. Their ignorance will be their undoing. Businesses need trained, educated people and new ideas. Educators and their institutions need money. When both parties unite in a win-win relationship, it's a match made in Heaven.

INVEST IN YOUR OWN CONTINUOUS IMPROVEMENT

I once heard Notre Dame football coach, Lou Holtz, remark that he had a lifetime coaching contract. "That means," he said, "that if we're leading at the end of the third quarter, I get to coach next week." Rapid changes in today's world are making iron-clad job security a very hard promise for businesses to keep. Every day, approximately 2,000 jobs disappear permanently from U.S. businesses. Companies that in the 1980s took pride in their no-lay-off policies have been forced to furlough employees for the first time in history. That's why it's important, no matter what you do for a living, to think of yourself as being in business for yourself.

While you may not have job security, you can create employment security. Employment security is achieved by sharpening your ability to learn and keeping up with latest and best ideas in your chosen field. As Cavett Robert, founder of the National Speakers Association, puts it, "School is never out for the pro."

But for too many of us, school has been out for a long time. Consider the following:

- Only three percent of all Americans own a library card.
- Fifty-eight percent of Americans will never read a nonfiction book after high school.
- The average American reads only one book per year of any kind.

- Only 14 percent of us visit a bookstore or library in a year.
- Only ten percent who buy a book will read past the first chapter.

Mark Twain said it best; "The man who doesn't read good books has no advantage over one who can't.

Learning how to learn is the ultimate employment security. If your job or occupation is eliminated, you simply choose another one and learn how to be the best you can be. That's why well-educated people who are in good health and willing to work rarely face chronic unemployment problems. They know how to learn. It's those without basic learning skills that face big-time problems in the new economy. As a Haitian proverb put it: "Ignorance doesn't kill you, but it makes you sweat a lot."

No matter what you want to learn or what field you work in, the good news is that there is plenty of information available. The bad news is that there is usually too much information available. Let's look at some basic strategies to help you find the best information sources and sharpen your learning skills.

Ask the Best

Start with this first strategy and you're almost guaranteed to get off on the right foot. It's a simple, commonsense idea and is the basic idea behind benchmarking. If you want to learn the best way to do something, find someone who does it extremely well and find out how they do it. Ask them where the best sources of information are and what skills are most important to master. Ask them questions such as:

- What are the most valuable lessons you've learned about being successful at this?

- What was most helpful to you when you were learning the ropes?
- What are the biggest mistakes to avoid and the greatest obstacles to overcome?
- Who else would you recommend I talk with?
- What books and periodicals should I be reading?
- Are there any courses in the field I should take?
- Are there any professional associations I need to join?
- What do you do to stay up to date?

It's been said that a person who wants to be rich should invite a rich person to dinner and pay for the meal. Successful people in almost every walk of life are usually accessible and willing to share much of what they know. All they ask is a sincere interest on your part and that you not take too much of their time.

Learning enables us to profit from the mistakes of others without having to experience the pain. So when you're trying to master something new, ask those who do it best. It usually costs little or nothing. They can direct you to the right sources. And you'll probably come away with a lot of great new ideas.

Recognize and Manage Learning Obstacles

Once you locate good information, the next step is to understand it so you can put it to work. In trying to understand new material, you're likely to confront one or more of the following three hurdles.

The first hurdle is unfamiliar words and terms. Whenever you are learning a new field of knowledge or a new technical skill, make it your business to learn all the jargon and unfamiliar words first. If you do that, the rest of the learning will go smoother and faster.

A second hurdle comes from skipping steps to learning. We

have to learn to crawl before we can walk and walk before we can run. Our mental processes work much the same way. For example, you can't learn algebra without a basic understanding of arithmetic, or learn calculus without knowing algebra. Similarly, you have to know how to write a sentence and structure a paragraph before you're ready to learn how to write a report. New learning is only possible if we begin with what we know and understand. Whenever you find yourself confused in trying to learn new material, go back to what you understand and move slowly forward from there.

A final hurdle comes from too much abstraction—you learn a lot of terms, definitions, and concepts but fail to see the value or how they apply to your job. For example, you're taking a course in statistical process control and the instructor is doing a bunch of calculations that seem abstract and meaningless. Raise your hand and ask, "Can you give me an example of how we can put this to work here?" If the instructor gets embarrassed because he can't give you one, that's his problem. The more specific examples and hands-on applications you can find, the better your grasp of the material will be. If you or the instructor can't find a useful application, why are you wasting your time?

According to A. J. Nock, "The mind is like the stomach. It is not how much you put into it that counts, but how much it digests." Overcoming learning obstacles is the antidote for learning indigestion.

Put What You Learn to Work

One of my favorite thoughts comes from an anonymous executive who said:

To look is one thing. To see what you look at is another. To understand what you see is a third. To learn from what you understand is still something else. But to act on what you learn is all that really matters.

No matter what the skill, there comes a time when you have to make the transition from pure learning to learning and doing. Let's use learning to play golf as an example. You can read all the books and magazines about golf. You can watch all the instructional videos about golf. You can interview golf pros, take lessons, and watch all the tournaments on television. But the only way you're going to benefit from what you've learned is to get on the course and start playing. Once you start playing, you learn which lessons are most valuable, where your strengths are, and where you need to improve.

When you learn a good idea or skill that works, you have two more things to do. First, see how many uses you can find for it. If you have learned to be computer literate, how many activities can you put on the computer that will save you and/or your company time and money? If you learn a good in-store promotion idea that works in Dallas, can you try it in Seattle or San Diego? Try to get maximum benefit from every new idea and skill you learn.

Second, teach what you've learned to those at work who can put the knowledge to good use. By doing this, you multiply the value of a skill or idea throughout the business. A great sales idea in the hands of a thousand salespersons is at least a thousand times more valuable than it was in the hands of one salesperson.

You're Never Too Busy to Learn

If you've read this far, I'm sure I'm preaching to the converted. No one in today's work world is too busy, too obligated, or too anything to invest in their own lifelong learning. When companies such as Corning and Motorola are mandating that all employees spend a minimum of 5 percent of company time in training, the message for the future is clear. Lifelong learning isn't a cultural nicety, it's an economic necessity. If you're too busy to learn, you won't be busy very long.

How many books and magazines are you reading each month to keep abreast of the latest developments and changes in your field? There's a lot of truth to the old cliché that "leaders are readers." Almost all the top business leaders I've met were voracious readers. They have an enormous amount of reading to do on the job Yet you see them getting on airplanes or leaving the office with several books in tow.

Too busy to read books? There are executive book-summary services that will send you four-page summaries of the most outstanding business books each month. Don't like to read? Nightingale-Conant and others publish audio-cassette programs and audio magazines on a wide variety of subjects by some of the best minds and experts in their respective fields. You can turn your dressing, driving, exercise, or shopping time into learning time and come away with an incredible number of ideas for improving your business and life.

The late Earl Nightingale claimed that if a person would only spend one hour a day learning about a particular subject, he or she would become a foremost expert on the subject within five years. Great thinkers and philosophers throughout the ages have repeatedly discovered what Earl called the strangest secret: "We become what we think about." Buddha was onto the secret when he said, "The mind is everything; what you think, you become." The Roman philosopher Marcus Aurelius was onto it when he wrote, "A man's life is what his thoughts make of it," as was Ralph Waldo Emerson when he said, "A man is what he thinks about all day long."

Tell me what you're learning and I'll tell you what you're becoming. So, here's a big question for you to ponder: What are you learning?

10 Just Do It!—Now!

Focused action beats intellectual brilliance every time in the marketplace of human affairs.

—MARK SANBORN

Think about the last time you had a tire changed at a service station. How long did you have to wait? Five minutes? Ten? Twenty?

Now think about this: It takes a pit crew at the Indianapolis 500 a few seconds to change a tire. There's a lot of money riding on doing the job fast and right. And that's how it gets done.

Which leads us to the final key to speed: expect it, demand it, and do it! Now! Don't let work expand to fill the time available. Instead, challenge yourself and others to reach your goals in a very short time and just do it.

Does it normally take four years to develop a new product and bring it to market? Set a two-year deadline and do it. That's what Hewlett-Packard did when it developed the Deskjet printer in only 22 months. Does it normally take three years to build a new factory? Set an 18-month deadline and do it. That's what Motorola did when it built an automated factory to manufacture electronic pagers. Do you try to respond to all customer inquiries within 24 hours? Set a deadline to respond within one hour and do it. Virtually all successful attempts to speed up the output of any business, store, department, team, process, or person begin with setting challenging goals, tight deadlines, and worshipping the schedule. As Al Bernstein remarked, "Sometimes the fool who rushes in gets the job done."

An executive once told me, "Completing a major project around here is like elephant breeding. At first, there's a lot of trumpeting, dirt throwing, and ground-shaking activity. Then nothing happens for almost two years." More often than not, when nothing happens, it's usually because goals and deadlines aren't clear, understood, or enforced. You can take steps to implement all the other nine commandments, but without deadlines nothing will happen. Setting clear goals and conforming to tight deadlines provide the necessary discipline and focus to turn ideas into action and dreams into reality. As Lord Herbert remarked, "The shortest answer is doing."

WHY TIGHT DEADLINES ARE SO IMPORTANT

The idea of setting deadlines is hardly new or revolutionary. But in today's rapidly changing world, setting tight, seemingly impossible deadlines is an essential ingredient to staying competitive. Being able to develop and market new products twice as fast as your competitors gives you a tremendous edge. Being the quickest to respond to a customer's inquiry or order gives you a tremendous edge. When you impose tough deadlines and get on with it, you're on your way to being the fastest, least-cost producer in your market.

Tight deadlines have become so important because they force us to make the necessary changes to survive in today's economy. Here's how they do it:

First, setting much tougher goals and deadlines creates a sense of urgency to find new ways to work smarter. Simply putting in more hours or working faster in the same old way isn't going to cut it. Meeting new standards forces us to rethink the way things are done and utilize the latest tools and techniques. Information technology becomes necessary. Management sheds layers and staff gets trimmed. Systems and processes are redesigned with time as the critical measure.

Second, tight deadlines leave no room for procrastination and delays in the system. Everyone knows that there's no time to put things off. Extraneous activities are squeezed out of the workday, and everyone is forced to concentrate their efforts on doing things that build value and contribute to finishing the job in the shortest possible time.

Third, if you're a manager, a tight deadline forces you to do the things that only you can do. There just isn't enough time to do everything yourself, so you're forced to train and empower others to do the rest. It builds a stronger organization, and good associates love it.

Finally, tight deadlines improve process quality. They force everyone to find a way to do things right the first time because that's the quickest way to get things done. As James F. Swallow, a Vice-President for consultant A. T. Kearney, put it, "Quality and cycle time is like the yin and the yang. If you go after cycle time, you lower the water level in your lake, and suddenly all the rocks stick out." The rocks, of course, are the places where mistakes and delays occur. Remove the rocks and both quality and speed improve.

When the entire organization works like this, the products get designed, produced, sold, and delivered much faster. The business becomes more customer responsive and service improves. Customers are happier, they buy more from you, and their numbers grow. Revenues go up and costs go down. The company makes a whole lot more money. And successful companies can provide more job security, job satisfaction, higher pay, and opportunities for growth. Once again, speed wins.

Is it easy? Hell no. It's very hard. But it can be an exciting adventure, and it's definitely worth it. And consider what will happen if your business clings to the same old goals and deadlines. If it hasn't already happened, sooner or later a fast-moving competitor will enter your market and start taking away your customers. Then in addition to losing money, your business is forced to play catch-up and make drastic changes to meet the competition. That's what Wal-Mart did to the likes of Sears and smaller, less fortunate retailers who went out of business. That's what Japanese auto manufacturers did to their U.S. counterparts. The choice is simple: Do you want to dictate the pace of your own change or have it dictated to you by someone who wants to put you out of business? Setting and meeting tough goals and deadlines is difficult in the short run but ultimately easier and far more profitable in the long run. Business, like life, is easiest on those who are tough on themselves.

INSTILLING THE "JUST DO IT!" ATTITUDE

As you read the previous two paragraphs you may have thought, "That's great, Michael. I agree with you, and Heaven knows we need to pick up the pace where I work. But how on earth am I going to get all those comfortable, complacent associates of mine to make the sacrifices necessary for such revolutionary change?" Since I don't know the people or where you work, I can't give you a precise answer. But I can give you some guidelines and examples of how others successfully do it.

At the most basic level, we spend our entire lives involved in two lifelong pursuits: seeking pleasure and avoiding pain. Virtually every act of human behavior is oriented toward fulfilling one or both of those two basic desires.

Pleasure and pain are the levers of change. People aren't going to change unless they perceive the status quo as threatening and/or the results of change as very rewarding. With that thought in mind, here are several guidelines for moving people from "business as usual" to the "just do it!" attitude.

1. EXPLAIN THE NECESSITY

Change is tough, and before people are willing to go through the discomfort of it they want to know why it's necessary and why *they* have to do it.

The more specific and graphic you can make your case for the necessity to change, the better. Are there new competitors entering your market? Are your customers making increased demands or buying elsewhere? Is your share of the market shrinking or growing more slowly? Do your major competitors respond faster, have new products or services, or cheaper prices? Muster all the charts, tables, graphs, and examples you can to make your case that it's a brand-new and rapidly changing world out there, and the era of business as usual is over. As Mike Walsh, CEO of Tenneco, put it, "You need to tell your people that if we do not change and change fundamentally, we are going out of business. And that will create insecurity. The trick is to turn that insecurity into positive tension."

2. Stress the Benefits

Once people understand that change is necessary, the next thing they need to know is what's in it for them. They don't care what's in it for the company, their boss, or the stockholders. They want to know how going through all this change and drastically improving their output is going to make their lives better. Will they have more money? More autonomy? More interesting and exciting work? Greater job security? A more important role to play? Greater opportunities for growth and personal satisfaction? Remember, you're selling people on the value of changing the way they work. And in every selling situation, people buy benefits. They need to know how the price they pay in time and effort will be more than offset by pleasures they will gain and the pain they will avoid. Here is an example of each:

When he arrived at Campbell Soup, CEO David Johnson asked his associates to focus achieving "20-20-20." That's his shorthand term for getting a 20 percent return in earnings growth, return on equity, and cash return on assets. To motivate them to focus on making the numbers, Johnson tells them, "If we deliver the 20-20-20, you're going to have the jingle jangle jingle in your pockets."

On the other hand, in trying to sell unionized auto workers on the idea of learning new skills and accepting flexible work rules at General Motors, UAW Vice President Donald Elphin took the pain-avoidance approach. "We're not helping GM," he said. "We're improving the product to sell cars and provide job security." He realized that it's difficult, if not impossible, to sell workers on the idea of helping an employer, which so many view as an adversary. Instead, he sold them on the idea of changing to save their jobs.

3. Aim High!

Successful leaders of change don't shuffle their feet by asking for gradual improvements. They put their best foot forward by asking for vast improvement in short order. And once those goals are achieved, even loftier ones are set. They realize that if you shoot for the moon, even if you fall short, you'll land among the stars. The following three examples illustrate how aiming high has paid off for Motorola, General Electric, and Hewlett-Packard.

In 1987, Motorola Chairman John Galvin said he wanted all cycle times and manufacturing defects reduced by 90 percent every five years. The same year Motorola also set a five-year goal to achieve what is known as the six-sigma level of quality, or no more than 3.4 defects per million components by 1992. They didn't reach six-sigma in '92. But during that five years, defects dropped from 6,000 per million to 30 per million. Not surprisingly, during the same five-year period, Motorola doubled its sales with only a slight increase in the work force. It also scored big wins in the global market. Japan's Nippon Telegraph and Telephone company bought over a million pagers from Motorola. When they reach the six-sigma level of quality, Motorola plans to shoot for a defect rate measured in parts per billion. Motorola knows that the way to stay ahead of the competition is to set tough goals, and then strive to break your own records.

In the early eighties, General Electric's circuit-breaker business was stagnating and facing stiff competition from abroad. The goal was set to reduce the elapsed time between a customer's order and delivery from three weeks to three days. Needless to say, achieving the goal took radical change. The number of plants producing circuit-breaker boxes was reduced from six to one. The plant in Salisbury, North Carolina, was automated. Decision making was speeded up by organizing the workforce into teams of 15 to 20, who made decisions on the factory floor. With workers making many of the decisions previously made by management, the number of management layers between plant manager and workers was cut from three to one. By the end of 1988, the goal of three days from order to delivery was achieved, along with a 30 percent decrease in manufacturing costs and a 20 percent increase in productivity.

Hewlett-Packard speeded up its business by challenging associates to cut break-even time in half. Break-even time is the interval from a new product's conception to when it begins making a profit. Halving break-even time is a very tall order that calls for totally redesigning the way things are done. And that's what H-P did.

Excess layers of management were cut. Product development was put under strong leaders who could cut through red tape and make fast decisions. The number of sites making personal computers was reduced from four to one. Laser printers, once shipped through hundreds of distribution centers worldwide, are now shipped through seven. Cost controls were tightened. Instead of a single sales force reporting to a huge bureaucracy, the sales force was divided and organized around products, with each salesperson reporting directly to those who design and manufacture the products they sell. The net result is that a once sluggish big company has transformed itself into a nimble giant.

4. Build Momentum With Breakthrough Projects

According to a Chinese proverb, "The man who removes a mountain begins by carrying away small stones." Similarly, you begin building a "just do it!" attitude by finding small, breakthrough projects with a good chance for success and just doing it. All the grand strategies in the world without action and tangible results are just a lot of hot air. As Henry Ford said, "You can't build a reputation on what you're going to do."

A good starting project is to ask everyone to focus on reducing cycle times—the time it takes to complete tasks. The concept is easy to understand, it produces quick results cheaply, and the impact on quality and productivity are highly visible. The key to reducing cycle times, according to Fred Wenninger of Iomega Corporation, is to "find your main bottleneck and attack it relentlessly." Wenninger should know. When he became Chief Executive at Iomega in 1989, the company was staggering from decreasing sales and a 1987 loss of $37 million. It took Iomega 28 days to produce a Bernoulli disc drive. By 1992, the production cycle time was reduced to only 1.5 days and the company earned a $14 million profit.

Another approach is to put together a team of passion... committed people to tackle a problem and use their success as a role model to build momentum. That's what Harley-Davidson did. From the early seventies to 1983, Harley's share of the U.S. heavy-motorcycle market plummeted from 100 to 23 percent, due to high-quality, low-cost competition from Japan. Almost bankrupt, Harley started its comeback with a "do it now!" philosophy and by carefully picking an improvement team. The team set the stage for the entire recovery. They defined problems, set milestones for achievement, and tried all the latest manufacturing and employee involvement techniques at a pilot plant. When the pilot plant was successful, Harley transformed all remaining plants into state-of-the art facilities. The manufacturing transformation, coupled with a new marketing campaign that targeted upscale buyers, has brought Harley-Davidson back from near death to one of the great business comeback stories of recent years.

5. It Takes Passion, Patience, and Persistence

The word is commitment. Someone or some group must believe passionately in the value of setting new goals and tighter deadlines. They must be willing to endure, encourage, inspire, armtwist, and cajole others until everyone understands the benefits of changing and the hazards of clinging to the status quo. Change without champions rarely, if ever, happens. As Thomas Gelb, Harley-Davidson's Vice President of manufacturing operations, remarked, "You can't delegate commitment. You have to feel it."

One way to keep people's energy up is to set short-term milestones for accomplishment and celebrate their achievement. For example, let's assume the goal is to reduce production cycle time by 50 percent. Whenever someone has an idea that eliminates a bottleneck or reduces cycle time in some way, recognize and reward it. Give them a public pat on the back or some token of appreciation and recognition. Another idea is to celebrate every time the cycle time is reduced by ten percent. You can have four small celebrations when the cycle time is reduced to 90, 80, 70, and 60 percent. Then have a big bash when the major goal is achieved.

Another good motivational technique is to recognize outstanding effort that demonstrates the "just do it!" attitude. For example, at Corning Inc., workers on a thermometer tubing team who went the extra mile for the customer told their story in a case presentation entitled, "Thrilling the Customer." In addition to giving the team members the public praise they deserve, the case gives associates a real-life example of the "just do it!" attitude in action. The following is a brief excerpt of their presentation:

> On February 16th, at 1:00 P.M., our Customer Service person received a call from a customer near Philadelphia. This customer was having a problem with our thermometer tubing in that the bore was fluctuating in size. They were in need of good glass in a hurry! . . . We knew that the trucking firms would take at least a day to get the glass to Philadelphia. We had a customer in trouble! Ron and I discussed the problem, and our solution was to take the product ourselves in the back of a station wagon. We got up at 2:00 A.M. and left by 3:00 A.M. We were waiting on the customer's dock when he arrived at 7:30. He was shocked and delighted.

That case also demonstrates another essential ingredient of the "just do it!" attitude. Work weeks aren't measured by hours. They're measured by achievement. The traditional attitude at most companies is, "I'll work hard for forty hours, but if I can't deliver what I promised, that's too bad. It can wait until next week." In a world where customers have so many choices, that can be a dangerous attitude. Instead, decide what you can accomplish and make good on your commitments. If it sometimes takes a 50- or 60-hour workweek, that's what it takes. If it means getting up in the wee hours on occasion to help a customer in trouble, that's what it takes. Today's market place is very unforgiving to those who can't keep commitments. Motorola defines the workweek as, "the time it takes to ship perfect product to the customer who's ordered it." In short, don't count the hours. Do whatever it takes to do the job right and on time.

HOW TO SPEED UP YOUR WORK WITHOUT RUINING YOUR LIFE

The story goes that a young woodsman challenged an older one to see who could chop the most wood in a single day. Throughout the day, the challenger worked fast and furiously, only stopping briefly for lunch. The older man worked at a steady pace, took a leisurely lunch, and several breaks during the day. At the end of the day, the challenger was stunned to see that his competitor had chopped considerably more wood.

"I don't get it," said the challenger. "Every time I looked up, you were taking a break. But you chopped more wood than I did."

"But what you didn't notice," said the winner, "was that I was sharpening my ax when I sat down to rest."

It's an old parable with an important message about work. Working harder and working smarter aren't the same things. Speeding up your work doesn't mean continuous busywork, buckets of sweat, and excessive hours on the job as a way of life. Unfortunately, that kind of behavior has become too common. It's counterproductive, hazardous to your health, and can literally kill you. The Japanese are so familiar with this phenomenon that they have a word for it. *Karoshi* means "death by overwork," most often from a heart attack. Actually, it isn't the work itself that kills. It's the negative stress created from feeling frustrated and fatigued. A 1972 U.S. medical study reported that the single best predictor of heart disease wasn't lack of exercise, high cholesterol, obesity, or smoking. It was job dissatisfaction.

Inasmuch as there's no such thing as a productive corpse, it's in everyone's best interest that you work smarter rather than harder. With that thought in mind, here are several strategies for speeding up your work with less stress.

1. Set Goals and Priorities

The formula for success in virtually any job, career, or activity can be summarized in two simple words: *focused persistence*. People who concentrate their time and energies on relentlessly pursuing one or a very few goals achieve the highest levels of success. After the pianist Paderewski gave one of his brilliant performances, a fan told him, "I'd give my life to play like that."

Paderewski replied, "I did."

The first key to speeding up your work is to know and write down your goals. Answer this question on paper: "What results am I trying to achieve and by when?" The more specific and measurable your goals are, the better. And be sure your goals have deadlines. If you have several goals, rank them in order of importance. Then resolve to spend the bulk of your time and energy on the few activities that contribute most to achieving your most important goals. This means having the self-discipline to say yes to relatively few activities and no to all the others. Whether you call it time management or self-management, getting more done in less time starts with setting goals and priorities.

2. Find Out Where You're Wasting Time

Next you need to learn how you are currently spending your time. Most of our time is spent in automatic, recurring patterns of behavior (habits). Some save time and others waste it. But we aren't aware of our habits until we make a conscious effort to identify them.

Keep a time log for a week. Write down every activity you engage in and how long it takes. At the end of the week, add up how much time was spent in each of your work activities. For example, if you're a salesperson, how much time did you spend on the telephone, in face-to-face contact with customers, traveling, attending meetings, dealing with interruptions, paperwork, and at lunch? Finding out where your time is actually going is usually a real eye opener. We don't realize the huge amount of time we waste on needless activities that don't contribute to achieving our goals. Most of us waste about half our time, and the best of us waste a good two hours each day.

Once you have completed the time-log exercise, sit down with the logs and your goals. Find a time and a quiet place where you can reflect and think without being interrupted. Then write down the answers to the following questions:

- What are my three greatest time wasters?
- How much time is being consumed by needless interruptions? Who or what is most responsible for them? How can they be minimized?
- What am I doing that's urgent but unimportant? How can these activities be reduced or eliminated?
- What are my most and least productive times of the day?
- Whom do I need to spend more time with? Whom do I need to see less of?
- What activities should I be devoting more time to?
- What activities should I be spending less time on?
- What activities can be eliminated or delegated?
- Am I trying to do too much?
- Am I procrastinating?
- What habits or tendencies are causing me to waste time?

3. Choose New Habits to Replace Old Ones

If you know your goals and priorities, complete the time-log exercise, and write the answers to the questions, then you have plenty of good ideas for accomplishing more in less time and with a lot less stress. All it takes is the willingness to replace time-wasting habits with productive ones.

For example, some years ago I assembled a list of 12 of the most common time wasters that plague us at work. Accompanying each time waster is a good, new habit to speed up your work:

Most Common Time Wasters

Time Waster	New Habit
1. Lack of Planning	1. Make a daily to-do list and rank items in order of importance. Then try to schedule your day to work on the most important tasks during prime time, the time of day when your energy is highest. That way, you give your best self to the most important tasks.
2. Paper Shuffling	2. Resolve to handle each piece of paper only once. Every time you pick up a piece of paper, either throw it away, file it, or do something to move it on its way.
3. Cluttered desk	3. Clear the top of your desk of everything except the item you're working on. If this isn't practical, resolve to clear your desk at the end of each work day.
4. Routine and trivia	4. Save trivial items and do them in batches. Do them in nonprime time when your energy level is low.

5. Trying to do too much	5. Don't do anything unnecessary or anything you can give to someone else. Practice saying no politely and rapidly. Slow down. The key to doing more is to do less better.
6. Afternoon Drowsiness	6. Eat a light lunch.
7. Too many interruptions	7. Establish a quiet time each day in which you can work undisturbed.
8. Drop-in visitors	8. Have visitors screened so you can see those you need to see. Close your door for part of the day. Schedule breaks and lunch hours to see those you need to see.
9. The telephone	9. Have calls screened or use voice mail to take incoming messages. Establish a time for placing and receiving calls. Put a three-minute hourglass by your telephone and try to complete calls in three minutes or less.
10. Meetings	10. Never go if you can send someone else. Establish starting and ending times. Schedule meetings back to back, before lunch, or at the end of the day.
11. Indecision	11. Accept risks as inevitable. Gather information, give yourself a deadline, and make a choice. That's what you're paid to do.
12. Procrastination	12. Break up that overwhelming job you're putting off into as many small jobs as you can. Give yourself a deadline for completing the entire project and work on it a little bit every day starting today.

Those are just a few of many ideas and techniques to help you get more out of each day. If you're interested in learning more about how you as an individual can get more done in less time, my book, *Working Smart* (published by Warner Books) and audio cassette program *Working Smarter* (published by Nightingale-Conant of Chicago) will give you a lot more information on the subject.

4. Have the Courage to Change and Just Do It!

The key to improving your personal output is to make first-rate habits second nature. Unfortunately, that's easier said than done. New habits don't feel comfortable at first, and we have to muster the willpower to practice them until they do. As runner Jim Ryan remarked, "Motivation is what gets you started. Habit is what keeps you going."

A good way to get started is to choose only one new habit and practice it without fail for three weeks. It normally takes three weeks for a new habit to feel comfortable. Once you're comfortable with the new habit, choose another, practice it for three weeks, choose another, and so on. Soon you'll find yourself getting a lot more done with a lot less stress. It's also very important that you begin immediately. If you wait until you feel inspired to begin, you'll wait forever. Just act the way you want to be and soon you'll be the way you act.

5. Be Disciplined But Flexible

One final word of caution. Don't become a time nut. Practicing any of these techniques in a rigid, mechanistic fashion is a blueprint for insanity and is counterproductive. Don't rigidly over-schedule your day with activities, because no day will go as planned. Running around with a stop watch and being compulsive about keeping a clear desk isn't going to make you more productive. It's a good practice to schedule quiet time to work alone. But common sense dictates that important customers and valued colleagues who need to see you will take precedence.

None of us can do all of these things all of the time, and life would be pretty dull if we did. But all of us can practice all of these habits some of the time. The key is to be aware of them and apply them with a healthy dose of flexibility and common sense. That's why having goals and priorities is so important. When you know what you're trying to accomplish, you can ask yourself "What's the best use of my time and energy right now?" The answer is usually obvious. Then you apply self-discipline and the right habits to make the best use of your time and energy. It's sometimes uncomfortable in the short run but ultimately much easier in the long run. Every achiever knows that delayed gratification and self-discipline is actually the easiest and best way to work, to live, and to get what you want out of life. Former British Prime Minister, Margaret Thatcher said it best:

> Look at a day when you are supremely satisfied at the end. It's not a day when you lounge around and do nothing. It's when you had everything to do and you did it.

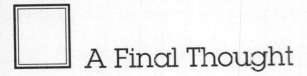 # A Final Thought

Two homeless men sat on a park bench discussing their unfortunate fate. "I'm here because I wouldn't listen to anybody," said the first.

"That's funny," said the second. "I'm here because I listened to everybody."

In a rapidly changing world, no one has all the right answers, because no one knows what the problems and opportunities will be. All we really know about the future is that things will be very different. To ignore change and carry on with business as usual is to react much like the first homeless man. To unquestionably follow what someone else tells us as gospel truth is to risk the fate of the second.

The job for all of us in business is to continuously listen, learn, *think*, and be prepared to capitalize on whatever the future brings. And that's precisely what I want you to get from this book. Instead of blindly following my ideas, think about them and choose the ones that you believe will help you most in your business and your career.

According to the late President John F. Kennedy, "Change is the law of life. And those who look only to the past and present are certain to miss the future." Whatever the future holds, this much is certain: With massive change comes incredible opportunity.

Once we know that, our job is to stay aware of what's happening and be prepared to act fast. Those who do will enjoy unprecedented success because when change is the problem, speed is the solution. Here's hoping that you and your team are among the fortunate fast.

 Postscript

What's Your Favorite Way to Win a Lot More Business in a Lot Less Time?

I hope this book has given you plenty of ideas for winning a lot more business in a lot less time. But if you have a unique idea that I didn't mention, or a great example, I would love to hear from you and possibly use it in my next book. Many of the ideas and anecdotes you read in this book came from readers who read my earlier books and were kind enough to pass them along.

What keeps you and your team focused on the customer? Have you discovered any good ways to make your business more flexible and quick to respond? Do you have any unique ways to get valuable feedback? Have you learned any ways to predict forthcoming changes in your business? Do you have any special ways to reduce waste or delays and make the best use of time? If so, please share them with me. Write and tell me the best, worst, most useful, and funniest business experiences that you know of. Type up your thoughts and send them to:

> Michael LeBoeuf
> P.O. Box 9504
> Metairie, LA 70055
> FAX: (504) 834-9478

Be sure to include your address and preferably a telephone number so I can contact you to verify the material if I decide to use it. In the event that I do, I'll send you a copy of the book and list your name in the acknowledgments, unless you wish to remain anonymous.

Thanks for sharing your experiences with me. And even if you have no experiences to share, I would still like to hear your thoughts. You're my customer, and I'm a great believer in the value of customer feedback.

Best regards,

Michael LeBoeuf

Index

Agility, 121, 123–24
Aid Association for Lutherans, 148, 158
Alaska Airlines, 105
American Express, 102
American Quality Foundation, 91
American Society for Training and Development (ASTD), 169
Apple Computer, 12
Arthur Andersen & Co.,124
AT&T, 174
Aubert, Fred, 86
Auto industry, U.S., 21, 26–28
Avon, 90–91

B

Baby boomers, 39, 46–47
Bank of America, 96
Baum, Neil, 87, 105, 110–11
Beals, Gary, 74
L.L. Bean, 91

Benchmarking, competitive, 90–91
Bernstein, Al, 190
Biotechnology, 37–38
Blank Arthur, 54
BMW, 182
Boeing, 59
Bureaucracy
    effects of, 146–47
    innovation and, 56
    value of eliminating, 144–45
Burnett, Bob, 166
Business Week, 167
Buying trends, capitalizing on customer, 43–49

C

Cadillac, 82
    See also Sewell Cadillac
Campbell Soup, 194
Canon, 59
Chang, Y. S., 87

Change
  benefits of, for employees,
    193–94
  commitment to, 197–99
  globalization and, 49–51
  guidelines for meeting,.192–99
  handling, 51–52
  impact on business, 40–43
  major trends, 38–40
  necessity for, 193
  putting it in perspective,
    35–38
  setting high goals for, 194–96
Chaparral Steel, 147, 148
Chrysler, 148, 151
Cincinnati Technical College,
  179
Citicorp, 48, 120
College Center of the Finger
  Lakes (CCFL), 179–80
Comment cards, 103–5
Competition, knowing your, 113–
  16
Complaints/errors, how to handle,
  86–87
Computers, impact of, 36–37
Convenience, importance of, 44
Corning, Inc., 80–81, 147, 158,
  168, 179–80, 198
Crosby, Phil, 90
Cusenza, John, 47
Customer(s)
  convenience, 44
  determining who are your, 102
  downsizing and input from,
    140–41

  effects of indirect contact with,
    30–31
  empathy, 29–30
  focus groups, 105
  hot lines, 111
  innovation and use of, 60–63
  internal, 32
  quality and expectations of,
    82–87
  staying focused on, 28–33
  treatment of, 29
Customer satisfaction and service
  examples of bad, 25–27
  examples of good, 19–20, 23–
    24. 27–28
  importance of, 20–24
  providing extras and, 83–85
  role of all employees in, 31–32
Customization, 42–43
Cypress Semiconductor Corp.,
  117

D

Dana Corp., 158
Deadlines
  guidelines for meeting, 192–99
  importance of tight, 189–192
Deming, W. Edwards, 87
Design-for-response, innovation
  and, 62–63
Dillard Department Stores, 132–
  33
Walt Disney World, 85
Domino's Pizza, 12, 78, 85

R. R. Donnelley & Sons, 43
Downsizing
 customer input and, 140–41
 eliminating bureaucracy
  versus, 144–45
 eliminating delays versus,
  142–43
 employee input and, 138–40
 problems with, 136–38
 simplicity and, 143–44
 use of process map for, 141–42
Drew, Richard, 60
Drucker, Peter, 56, 66

E

Eastern Airlines, 26, 101
Eastman Kodak, 43
Economic growth, role of
  business/education
  partnerships and, 181–83
Education
 and practical applications,
  186–87
 customized courses, 179–80
 economic growth and, 181–83
 importance of, 166–68
 learning obstacles, 185–86
 on-the-job learning, 168–76
 pay-for-knowledge, 172–74
 retraining through cooperative,
  178–79
 role of businesses and colleges,
  180–83
 self-directed learning, 174–76

sources of information,
  184–85
 taking the time for, 187–88
 training versus, 169–70
 workplace literacy, 170–72
 youth apprenticeship programs,
  177–78
Effectiveness Dimensions, Inc.,
  154
Einstein, Albert, 70
Electronic Data Systems (EDS),
  135
Elphin Donald, 194
Embassy Suites, 173
Emerson, Ralph Waldo, 124, 188
Employment security, 183–84
Empowerment, employee, 128–
  29, 149–54
Environmentalism, 47
Ernst & Young, 91
Experts, innovation and, 55–56

F

Federal Express, 12, 31–32, 85,
  88, 147, 173–74, 175
Feedback
 comment cards and, 103–5
 customer hot lines and, 111
 customer letters and, 101–2
 focus groups and, 105
 from ex-customers, 112–13
 how to obtain, 97
 mystery shoppers and, 105,
  110–11

Feedback (*continued*)
  obtaining useful information,
    98–101
  from peers/subordinates, 118
  performance and, 116–19
  reason for, 94–96
  from suppliers, 118–19
  surveys and, 103, 105
  tracking sales and, 111–12
Feigenbaum, Armand, 140
Financial concerns, innovation
    and, 55
First National Bank of Chicago,
    144–45
Focus groups
  feedback and, 105
  innovation and, 61–62
Ford, Henry, 57, 196
Ford Motor Co., 91
Frito-Lay, 42

G

Galvin, John, 194–95
Gates, Bill, 47–48, 128
Gelb, Thomas, 197
Geneen, Harold, 96
General Electric, 45, 57, 67–68,
    131–32, 133, 142, 147, 195
General Mills, 148
General Motors, 48, 57, 81, 97,
    122, 135, 148, 171, 194
Globalization, impact of, 49–51
Goal setting, 194–96, 200
Grann, Phyllis, 29–30

Gray power (power of the aging
    population), 38
Gremer, John, 84
Grune, George, 30

H

Hanes, John, 154
Hannah, Jim, 25, 33
Harley-Davidson, 197
Hart-Marx Clothing, 86
Harvard Business Review, 23
Henderson, Terry, 171
Hewlett-Packard, 59, 65, 120,
    189, 195–96
Holiday Inn, 49
Holtz, Lou, 183
Home Depot, 45, 54
Honda, 59
Hoser, Albert, 128
Houghton, James R., 80–81
Human nature, innovation and,
    54

I

IBM, 40, 64
Idea-generating cycle, 69–70
Information
  factual, 99
  obtaining useful, 98–101
  timely, 99–100
Innovation
  barriers to, 54–57

creative prototyping and, 62
design-for-response and, 62–
63
focus groups and, 61–62
how to create and harvest
ideas, 68–75
job insecurity and, 55
need for continuous, 53–54
Innovation strategies
building from core
competencies, 59–60
creating an innovative climate,
64–68
demanding and expecting
innovation, 58–59
using customers to create, 60–
63
using small entrepreneurial
teams, 63–64
Intel, 59
Interactive video disc (IVD),
174–75
Iomega Corp., 196
ITT, 96

J

James, William, 71
Jefferson Smurfit Corp., 133
Job insecurity, innovation and,
55
Johnson, David, 194
Johnson & Johnson, 58–59, 92
Johnsonville Foods, 148, 175–76
Juran, Joseph, 77

K

Karoshi, 199
A. T. Kearney, 191
Kelleher, Herb, 101
Kennedy, John F., 207
Kettering, Charles, 56
Kindred, David, 99
K-Mart, 114
Kroc, Ray, 71

L

Labovitz, George, 87
Lawsuits, employee, 138
Learning, on-the-job. *See*
Training
Learning Curve, 175
Learning obstacles, 185–86
Lifestyles, changes in, 39–40, 44
Literacy, workplace, 170–72

M

Mac Connection, 120–21
McDonald's, 71
McGraw-Hill, 43
McLuhan, Marshall, 36, 72
Macy's, 49
Malcolm Baldrige National
Quality Award, 82, 89, 93
Management
by objectives, 117
employee empowerment and,
128–29, 149–54

Management (*continued*)
    teamwork and role of middle,
        164–65
    traditional style of, 148–49
Marcus, Bernard, 54
Marriott, Bill, Jr., 97
Marriott Corp., 33
Matsushita, 88
Mayer, Louis B., 118
Medical Alley, 182
Merck & Co., Inc., 57, 59
Meredith Corp., 166
Microsoft Corp., 47–48, 128
Middle-class market, shrinking,
        48–49
Milliken & Co., 132–33
Mitchell & Co., 137
Motorola, 59, 88–89, 91, 120,
        168, 170–71, 180–81, 189,
        194–95, 199

N

National, 121
National Association of
        Accountants, 140
National Association of
        Suggestion Systems, 92
Nightingale, Earl, 50–51,
        188
Nightingale-Conant Corp., 32,
        188, 204
Nippon Telegraph and Telephone,
        195
Nock, A. J., 186

Nordstrom, 24, 49
Northwestern University, 180–81

O

Office Depot, 45
Official Airlines Guide (OAG),
        48
One-Idea Club Hall of Fame, 73
Ono, Taiichi, 91
On-the-job learning. *See* Training

P

Parkinson, C. Northcote, 135
Partnering, 130–33
Pauling, Linus, 72
Pay-for-knowledge, 172–74
Peers, feedback from, 118
J. C. Penney, 49
Perceived quality, 79
Performance feedback, 116–19
Perot, H. Ross, 67, 135
Piccinini, Miriam, 33
Popcorn, Faith, 34
Popcorn Report, The (Popcorn),
        34
Price, Sol, 115
Price Club, 115
Princeton Corridor, 182
Process map, 141–42
Process quality, 78
Procter & Gamble, 100, 130–31,
        148

Prototyping, innovation and, 62
Putnam Berkley Group, Inc., 29

Q

Quality
  benefits from providing, 76–78
  costs, 87–89, 90
  customer expectations and,
    82–87
  importance of commitment to,
    80–81
  -improvement teams, 89–90,
    92
  improving by involving
    employees, 81–82
  perceived, 79
  problems with some programs,
    91–93
  process, 78
  providing extras to customers
    and, 83– 85
  total quality management, 79
Quick-Response partnerships,
  132–33, 134
Quotron, 48

R

Ralston Purina Co., 34
Ramada Inn, 49
Rath, Duane, 24–25
Rath Manufacturing Co., 24
Reader's Digest, 30

Reichheld, Frederick E.. 23
Research Triangle, 181
Responsiveness
  company size and, 121–22
  developing core strengths,
    130–33
  employee empowerment and,
    128–29
  examples of, 120–21
  partnering, 130–33
  specialization and, 125–27
  speed vs. cost and, 124–25
  streamlining and, 127–28
  technology and, 133–34
  what doesn't work, 122–23
  what works, 123–34
Rewards, teamwork, 161–62
Richards, Tony, 30, 33
Rigsbee, Ed, 74
Robert, Cavett, 183
Robert Bosch Corp., 178
Rodgers, T. J., 117
Route 128 (Boston), 131
Rubbermaid, Inc., 57, 58, 64
Ryan, Jim, 204

S

Sam's Club, 112, 115
Sanders, Jerry, 171
Sasser, W. Earl, Jr., 23
Saturn, 158
Schrage, Michael, 93
Sea-Land Services, 139–40
Sealtest, 49

Sears, 49, 114, 178
Sebastian International, 47
Seiko, 62
Self-directed learning, 174–76
Service
  guarantee, 85–86
  See also Customer satisfaction
    and service
Sewell, Carl, 20, 21
Sewell Cadillac, 83, 103, 105
Shaw, George Bernard, 65–66
Shenandoah Life Insurance Co.,
  148, 173
Siemens, 128
Silicon Hills, 182
Silicon Valley, 181
Skills needed for teamwork, 157–
  58
Sloan, Alfred, 97
Slutsky, Jeff, 74
Smith, Adam, 125
Smith, Fred, 77
Sony, 62–63
Southwest Airlines, 45, 101–2,
  142–43
Specialization, 125–27
Speed
  importance of, 12–13
  ten commandments of, 14
  without stress, 199–205
Stayer, Ralph, 148
Steelcase, Inc., 175
Steering committee, use of, 155–
  56
Steinbeck, John, 71
Stiritz, William, 34

Stress, speed without, 199–205
Subordinates, feedback from, 118
Success, innovation and, 56–57
Suppliers, feedback from, 118–19
Surveys, customer, 103, 105
Swallow, James F., 191

T

Taco Bell, 45
Teamwork
  determining if it will work in
    your business, 152–54
  effectiveness of, 151–52
  employee empowerment, 128–
    29, 149–54
  examples of, 147–48
  self-directed, 150–51
  skills needed for, 157–58
Teamwork, how to create
  gradual degrees of
    empowerment, 163–64
  role of middle management,
    164–65
  role of training, 156–58
  selecting sites for, 158–59
  stages of, 159–61
  use of rewards, 161–62
  use of a steering committee,
    155–56
Technology
  impact of, 11, 36–38
  responsiveness and, 133–34
  major trends, 38–40
TGI Friday's Restaurants, 30

Thatcher, Margaret, 205
Thomas, George, 71
Thornton, Robert, 73
3M, 57, 58, 59, 60, 62, 65, 66, 68, 72, 128, 147
Thurow, Lester, 167–68
Time
    discipline and flexibility and, 204–5
    minimizing perceived waiting, 85
    value of, 44
    wasters, 202–3
Time log, use of, 201
Total quality management (TQM), 79
Toyota, 59
Training
    cooperative education and retraining, 178–79
    costs of, 168
    education versus, 169–70
    pay-for-knowledge, 172–74
    self-directed learning, 174–76
    teamwork and, 156–58
    workplace literacy, 170–72
TV Guide, 48

U

U.S. General Accounting Office, 93
United States Surgical, 61

University of Michigan, 138
University of Texas, 182

V

Value
    adding, 136
    eliminating bureaucracy and, 144–45
    eliminating delays and, 142–43
    employee input and, 138–40
    paying for, 45
    simplicity and, 143–44
von Hippel, Eric, 60

W

Wal-Mart, 45, 49, 65, 83–84, 86, 97, 112, 114, 120, 130–31, 133–34, 192
Walsh, Mike, 193
Walton, Sam, 85, 97, 115
Wang, An, 96
Warren Featherbone, 132–33, 134
Watson, Thomas, Jr., 64
Welch, Jack, 45, 142
Wenninger, Fred, 196
Whalen, Charles, 134
Whitney, Eli, 71
Work force
    diversity, 39
    See also Teamwork
Work hours, increase in, 44

Wright, Ron, 75
Wyatt Co., 136–37, 138

X

Xerox, 90, 91

Y

Yankelovich, Daniel, 81
Yates, Ron, 133
Youth apprenticeship programs,
    177–78

About the Author

Companies ranging from Fortune 500–sized corporations to small banks and medical practices turn to Dr. Michael LeBoeuf when they want solid, practical ways to live and work smarter. He is an internationally published author, business consultant, and a dynamic professional speaker and seminar leader. A former university professor, Dr. LeBoeuf received his Ph.D. from Louisiana State University. He taught courses in management, organizational behavior, and communication at the University of New Orleans for twenty years, retiring as Professor Emeritus in 1989.

His previous books, *Working Smart, Imagineering, GMP: The Greatest Management Principle in the World*, and *How to Win Customers and Keep Them for Life*, have been published in over a dozen different languages, selected by major book clubs, and excerpted in newspapers and magazines on all continents. In addition, his books have been adapted to produce several best-selling audio-cassette and video-training programs.

In constant demand as a speaker, Dr. LeBoeuf addresses business and professional audiences worldwide. He has appeared on hundreds of radio and television shows including *Good Morning America* and the *CBS Evening News*. As both a speaker and a writer, his ability to communicate with clarity and enthusiasm make him a popular favorite.

221